More praise for *The Art of Connection*

"Leadership is all about developing a culture that supports collaboration, innovation, and high performance. The heart of what's really required to make that happen is brought to life in this artful book. It is filled with motivational strategies and practical guidance to help you connect with yourself and others. If you lead any kind of team that aspires to greatness, you'll want to be sure everyone reads *The Art of Connection*. Great stuff!"

— **Dennis Mannion,** former president and CEO of the
Los Angeles Dodgers and Detroit Pistons

"There are many excellent books on leadership, communication, and relationships that offer all kinds of tips on how to get along with others, but this book goes deeper. Michael Gelb guides us to discover the surprising connections between our relationship skills and our happiness, health, and effectiveness, both professionally and personally. He illuminates the essential inner work we all must do if we want to thrive as conscious, compassionate leaders, but he manages to deal with these profound issues in a way that is fun, engaging, and, not surprisingly, creative!"

— **Karen Page,** former chair of the Harvard Business School
Alumnae Association, two-time winner of the James Beard Award,
and author of *The Flavor Bible* and *Kitchen Creativity*

"An important book on an essential topic. I appreciate Gelb's blend of storytelling, practical lessons, and cutting-edge science. Connection may be *the* most important skill for leaders, and for all humans, to embrace and cultivate."

— **Marc Lesser,** author of *Less: Accomplishing More by Doing Less*

"Many people have a belief in, and perhaps even a feel for, the interconnectedness of life but find it challenging to walk the talk by applying that to their relationships, both at work and at home. In this enlightening, urgently needed, and wonderfully entertaining book, Michael Gelb creatively bridges the gap between our natural intuitive wisdom and the application of such into our everyday lives. By learning the seven

life-changing skills shared in *The Art of Connection*, readers can begin to develop powerful habits that raise their core energy. The result? Positive, mutually supportive, and highly conscious relationships. A must-read for coaches and leaders at all levels, as well as for anyone who wants to take their personal connections with others to the next level."

— **Bruce D Schneider,** founder of iPEC Coaching and author of *Energy Leadership: Transforming Your Workplace and Your Life from the Core*

"Michael Gelb is a genius at helping others discover and express their creative potential. Now, in this precious, profound book, he guides us to develop the skills of emotional, spiritual, and practical intelligence that we all need to translate creative ideas into action."

— **Tony Buzan,** originator of Mind Mapping

"Truly a brilliant book! I have continually witnessed the ways in which camaraderie and connection allow a workplace and its surrounding community to thrive. Communication *is* leadership. In *The Art of Connection*, Gelb brilliantly instructs us how to communicate in a compassionate and genuine manner in order to build relationships that allow us and those around us to flourish. The book is an ideal guide for conscious leaders or any individuals aiming to improve their relationships with others, and, by doing so, more positively impact the world."

— **Kip Tindell,** former CEO and co-chairman of The Container Store

"Michael Gelb is the premier voice on creativity for the coaching profession. And, as he explains in this fabulous new book, the most powerful catalyst for inspiring creative breakthroughs and translating those breakthroughs into sustainable innovations is to connect with other people first, before trying to solve a problem. In these pages he lays out a clear and practical path for cultivating the relationship-building skills that *everyone* needs now!"

— **Dr. Marcia Reynolds,** past president of ICF Global Board and author of *The Discomfort Zone*

THE ART OF CONNECTION

THE ART OF CONNECTION

7 RELATIONSHIP-BUILDING SKILLS
EVERY LEADER NEEDS *NOW*

MICHAEL J. GELB

New World Library
Novato, California

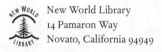

New World Library
14 Pamaron Way
Novato, California 94949

Some of the ideas, examples, and exercises in this book appeared in different forms in *Thinking for a Change* and other works by the author. They are reframed and contextualized here to be most useful and relevant to our present circumstances.

Text design by Megan Colman

Library of Congress Cataloging-in-Publication Data
Names: Gelb, Michael J., author.
Title: The art of connection : 7 relationship-building skills every leader needs now / Michael J. Gelb.
Description: Novato, California : New World Library, [2017] | Includes index.
Identifiers: LCCN 2017018861 (print) | LCCN 2017033271 (ebook) | ISBN 9781608684502 (Ebook) | ISBN 9781608684496 (alk. paper)
Subjects: LCSH: Leadership. | Interpersonal relations. | Organizational behavior.
Classification: LCC HD57.7 (ebook) | LCC HD57.7 .G4497 2017 (print) | DDC 658.4/092—dc23
LC record available at https://lccn.loc.gov/2017018861

First printing, September 2017
ISBN 978-1-60868-449-6
Ebook ISBN 978-1-60868-450-2
Printed in Canada on 100% postconsumer-waste recycled paper

New World Library is proud to be a Gold Certified Environmentally Responsible Publisher. Publisher certification awarded by Green Press Initiative. www.greenpressinitiative.org

10   9   8   7   6   5   4   3   2   1

*This book is dedicated to helping you develop
the relationship-building skills you will need to lead us to
a more creative, enlightened, and compassionate world.*

Contents

Prologue

Wheels Up

"We're probably the people with the lowest combined GPA and SAT scores who've ever sold a company to Warren Buffett!" quipped Gary Spitalnik, EVP of Wheels Up, a membership-based private aviation company. He laughed uproariously as he explained how he and his friends played a role in the sale of Marquis Jet to NetJets, part of Buffett's Berkshire Hathaway empire. Gary's warmth and genuine friendliness filled the room when we met at a recent business dinner in Houston. I had just flown in to give a speech and was feeling a bit tired, but his questions and ability to listen to my responses buoyed my energy and inspired my curiosity. As he and his colleagues explained the vision behind their innovative entrepreneurial venture — "democratizing private jet travel" — they also shared how much fun they were having at work. Gary enthused, "Our business is all about connecting with people. We love it!"

When I mentioned that I was writing a book entitled *The Art of Connection*, he jumped out of his chair and exclaimed, "That's us! That's what we are all about. Wait until you meet Kenny."

Spitalnik's enthusiasm rose to another level as he spoke about Kenny Dichter, the CEO of Wheels Up and cofounder of Marquis Jet and Tequila Avión (featured on the HBO series *Entourage* and winner of the "Best Tequila in the World" award at the San Francisco World Spirits Competition).

As an article in *Entrepreneur* magazine states: "Kenny Dichter is someone you want to know, and he wants to know you, too. No, he really does." Kenny's wife and business partner, Shoshana, adds that her husband's success is a "reflection of his gift for connecting with people." She says, "He's a master at building relationships."

The crew at Wheels Up exemplifies many of the skills that we will be exploring. Its leaders transmit a positive energy that is uplifting and contagious. When you interact with any kind of organization, you can usually get a sense of the skill of the leaders based on the energy. When the energy is low and weak, chances are the leadership is poor. When the energy is positive and strong, odds are so is the leadership. This manifests in all kinds of ways, from the largest gestures down to the smallest details. The greeting by the host at a restaurant, the reception at the hotel check-in, and the interaction with a gate agent at an airline all convey powerful messages, for better or worse, about the quality of leadership.

In the course of more than three decades of consulting with organizations around the world, I've seen the best and the worst of workplaces. All of the best places are characterized by a sense of camaraderie and connection. This isn't the only factor in a successful endeavor, but it is a critical one.

My career has been built on developing energizing, enduring connections with visionary, positive leaders. When I began leading seminars for executives, I was the youngest person in the room, and now I'm usually the oldest. My passion for helping emerging leaders learn the skills they need is greater than ever.

What are those skills, and how have they changed? Many of the essentials skills remain unchanged, but others have evolved considerably due to rapidly changing circumstances. The most important shifts include new currencies, free agency, and a more horizontal structure in which diversity, collaboration, and intrinsic incentives play larger roles.

Attention and personal energy are the new currencies. Ten years ago the companies with the largest market capitalization were mostly oil companies, and today they are organizations focused on capturing and selling attention via advertising (Google, Facebook, etc.). The ability to connect with others, to engage their attention, is more important now than ever before. And energy management has replaced time management. When I began my career, "time-management seminars" were ubiquitous. Now these programs are mostly extinct. Professor James Clawson, author of *Level Three Leadership: Getting Below the Surface*, heralded this shift when he wrote in 1999: "Leadership is about managing energy, first in yourself and then in others."

We are all free agents. On October 22, 2003, my seminar for regional managers at a multinational pharmaceutical company was interrupted by a special address from the CEO. We were summoned to the cafeteria, where we watched a webcast in which he announced that 4,400 people would lose their jobs in what turned out to be the first of a series of major restructurings. After the shocking news, I asked the group if they wanted to continue with the program or return to their offices. They voted to continue. As one manager stated, "What we are learning is exactly what we need to deal with these challenging circumstances."

Many large companies like AT&T, Boeing, DuPont, IBM, and Merck, which used to be stable places to work, have changed dramatically over the years. Most of the visionary leaders with whom I collaborated at these companies have moved on to other opportunities, and many of them are my clients in their new roles. All of them are gifted in many ways, but the distinguishing attribute of the finest leaders is their skill in building relationships.

The concept of a "job" is obsolete. You may have a position at a company, but that could end tomorrow. You are a free agent, the leader of your own enterprise. If you are employed by a company now, it just means that you have only one client. If you lose that position tomorrow, it is your *relationships* that will help you manage the transition successfully.

The workforce is more diverse and less hierarchical, collaboration is more important, and the best people are more motivated by intrinsic incentives. Our society is more diverse and business is more global, so leaders need to be more flexible and adaptable in their relationship-building and communication skills. Teams form, accomplish a task, and then reform for a new task. Collaboration has always been important, but now teams must come together to build trust and alignment faster than ever. Money is still important as a reward, but increasingly so is a sense of meaning, purpose, and connection. Guiding others to discover a sense of meaning, purpose, and connection is an increasingly important element of contemporary leadership.

Much of what follows is drawn from leadership development seminars I've designed and conducted for clients in many different organizations, large and small, profit and nonprofit. Each seminar begins with a few questions for contemplation and then clarification of some fundamental definitions and underlying assumptions, followed by setting goals for our time together. Let's do that here as well.

What Is Leadership?

There seem to be as many different definitions and descriptions of leaders and leadership as there are leadership books. Before I share mine, please consider yours.

What's your definition of leadership?
What are the most important qualities and skills that leaders
    need now?

Have the skills leaders need changed?
How does leadership differ from management?
Does leadership require charisma?
Is leadership dependent on title, office, or position?
Are leaders born or made?

Here is my formal definition of leadership:

> Leadership is a process of social influence that optimizes
> the energy of others to realize a vision,
> execute a strategy, or achieve a goal.

My informal definition is:

> Leadership is the art of connection! It's about building
> relationships to bring out the best in others.

At Wheels Up and in every organization where the atmosphere is infused with positive energy, the leaders are skilled in relationship building. As you improve your skills in connecting with others, you're more likely to be recognized as a leader. As you gain recognition and become more senior in an organization, people watch you and the way you treat others with hawklike attention. In companies, schools, nonprofit organizations, and at home, leaders set the example of connection and take responsibility for the quality of relationships, which determines the quality of energy.

Three Myths about Leadership

Before we go further, let's examine three common misconceptions about what it takes to be a leader.

1. *Leadership is a function of position, title, or seniority.* Leadership skills used to be thought of as just for those at the top of

the pyramid, but as organizations become less hierarchical, these skills become more important for everyone. Although leadership isn't necessarily correlated with position, title, or seniority, if you have gained responsibility or are in a position of formal authority, it's even more important to refine these skills.

2. *Leadership requires charisma and extroversion.* Charisma can be useful in inspiring people to "buy into" a vision, but it's not necessary. What is necessary, whether you're an extrovert, introvert, or ambivert, is self-awareness and openness to change. For charismatic extroverts this often means being more receptive and empathic, and for shy introverts it means learning to be more social and assertive.

3. *Leaders are born, not made.* The idea that leadership is determined genetically is, as pioneering scholar and consultant Warren Bennis (1925–2014) emphasized, the most dangerous leadership myth. It's dangerous because it stops many people from cultivating the skills they need to lead. Bennis exhorts: "This myth asserts that people simply either have certain charismatic qualities or not. That's nonsense; in fact, the opposite is true." He concludes, "Leaders are made rather than born."

How do you make yourself into a leader? You learn the skills of the art of connection. Sam Horn offers a compelling example. She's a leader with remarkable relationship-building skills, a role model for anyone interested in the art of connection. Acclaimed as the "Intrigue Expert," she's an internationally renowned communications strategist who has written a number of bestsellers and coached many of the world's top entrepreneurs and executives. Sam brings people together to bring out their best. Just one example: she helped create the Maui Writers Conference and was its executive director and seventeen-time emcee.

But what makes her such a compelling role model for leaders who want to develop their relationship-building skills is that she wasn't "born" with this gift; she made it happen. As she expresses it: "I was a smart girl in a small town, and being a smart girl in a small town is *not* a prescription for popularity. I was a brainiac with little patience for small talk. I loved talking about big ideas. At the time, I didn't realize that sometimes comes across as showing off."

When Sam was fifteen years old, she discovered Dale Carnegie's classic book *How to Win Friends and Influence People* (1936). Her life changed forever when she read these words: "You can make more friends in two months by becoming interested in other people than you can in two years by trying to get other people interested in you." Sam realized that instead of showing off and trying to be the most interesting person in the room, she could train herself to be the most *interested* person in the room. She explains, "Instead of talking about what I know, I focus on finding out what other people know." Sam, who now usually becomes the most popular woman in any room she enters, attributes her success to her continuing quest to improve her relationship-building skills. She enthuses, "Connection is the secret of life!"

Leaders are made, not born, and the making is a process that continues throughout life. This has not changed. Except, perhaps, that it has become more important.

How Does Leadership Differ from Management?

Leadership is the art of accomplishing more than
the science of management says is possible.
— COLIN POWELL, former U.S. Secretary of State

Managers are busy cutting their way through the forest. The leader climbs the tallest tree, looks around, and shouts, "Hey, we're cutting through the wrong forest." The managers respond, "Shut up! We're making progress!"

Managers control, organize, and measure. Leaders strategize, inspire, and energize. In the real world, now *we must all do both*! We all have to sharpen our saws and help cut through the forest *and* remain cognizant of the big picture and the purpose of our actions, while consistently striving to bring out the best in ourselves and others.

In the past managers were asked to focus on doing things right, whereas leaders put more emphasis on doing the right things. Now we must all focus on doing the right things right.

Becoming a Conscious Leader

Please take a few minutes to contemplate these three questions:

1. What percentage of people's visible behavior do you think is habitual? In other words, as you watch people go about their everyday activities — entering an elevator, queuing up at an airline check-in counter, ordering a latte — how much of what they're doing is on automatic pilot?

2. What percentage of people's internal dialogue do you think is habitual? In other words, as you watch people go about their everyday activities, how much of their self-talk, or internal conversation, is on automatic pilot?

3. What percentage of people's values, assumptions, beliefs, and expectations (VABEs) do you think is habitual? In other words, how aware are people of the deeper motivations underlying their behaviors and accompanying internal dialogue?

Jim Clawson begins our seminar at the Darden Graduate School of Business by posing these three questions to our group of executives. Jim and I have taught this "Leading Innovation" program together for more than ten years, and each time these questions stimulate lively conversation. In every class the somewhat surprising consensus is that most people are functioning on automatic pilot most of the time. The last class agreed that at least 80 percent of visible behavior and 80 percent of internal dialogue were proceeding unconsciously and that a whopping 98 percent of people's deeper motivations was playing out below the surface of their consciousness.

In the industrial age many organizations were influenced by behaviorism, a school of psychology based on the idea that all that matters is what can be observed and measured. Behaviorists aim to reinforce behaviors deemed desirable through reward, or "positive reinforcement," and discourage those deemed undesirable through punishment, or "negative reinforcement." Clawson refers to the attempt to manipulate visible behavior as Level One, and his research over decades shows that it usually doesn't work very well. Rather than causing people to buy into a change or innovation, the carrot-and-stick approach may compel short-term compliance, but frequently results in either active or passive resistance.

Level Two is the realm of appealing to people's internal dialogue through reason, data, and argument. When the CEO cited earlier gave his webcast announcing the force reduction, he offered a carefully considered, well-reasoned case for its necessity. Many large corporations operate on this level, and what they get, according to Clawson's research, is either apathy, compliance, or at best agreement.

At Level Three the appeal is to people's deeper motivations and sense of higher purpose. Level Three leadership is the art of connecting with others to liberate creative energy by aligning values, assumptions, beliefs, and expectations (VABEs). Like a good therapist, a Level Three leader needs to understand and be able to communicate about VABEs. Clawson's research demonstrates that aligned VABEs are the drivers of sustainable world-class performance. Great organizations are characterized by a sense of engagement, and even passion, that stems from the energy unleashed when people care deeply about what they're doing and why they're doing it.

In the contemporary world of work the best people are more aware of their options and much more motivated by a sense of meaning, purpose, and connectedness than in any previous generation. Level Three leaders, those who are capable of building relationships by connecting with people "beneath the surface," are increasingly valuable to organizations who want to attract and keep high performers.

You don't become a psychotherapist without going through therapy yourself, and you don't become a Level Three leader without conscious consideration of your own VABEs. Most people are relatively unaware and avoid considering their values, assumptions, beliefs, and expectations until they're forced to by illness, death of a loved one, divorce, or some other trauma.

Don't wait! History's greatest leaders have always operated from Level Three. *Now you can too.*

The Soul Impetus

In the 1970s managers were managers. In the 1980s managers were asked to learn how to be leaders, something that has become more important every decade since. In the first decade of the new millennium, managers were also asked to develop the skill of coaches. Now if you work in any kind of organization, in addition to knowing how to be a coach, it really helps if you can think and speak like a psychotherapist. The same thing is true for parents and spouses.

I first learned how to speak like a therapist from my mom, Joan, who worked for years at the Passaic County Mental Health Clinic. After raising me, her work treating sociopaths, addicts, and murderers seemed easy. Joan has a special gift for connecting with people, which served her well at home and in her work. She recounts:

One of my regular patients, Anita, was only twenty-four years old, but she weighed more than three hundred pounds and was on ten years' probation for threatening to blow up the post office (a federal offense). She had a long history of assaultive behavior. I saw her once a week for about three years, and we built a solid relationship.

One day she came in highly agitated and couldn't say what had upset her. All of a sudden, she jumped up and shouted, "Joan, get out of the room fast! I'm going to tear this office apart. Get out NOW!" I did, and it was a good thing, as she trashed the office completely before being dragged away by the police. I was touched by the way she communicated her trust in me. She knew that I cared for her, and in the midst of acting out her rage she remembered our connection. (Incidentally, I was using another office that day while mine was being painted!)

My dad, Sandy, retired from his oral surgery practice almost twenty years ago, but people still remember him fondly. The reason is that, besides being a superb and dedicated technician, he cared about his patients. Without ever being a "touchy-feely" type, he calmed the fears of patients facing extractions of impacted wisdom teeth or reconstructive surgery. Sandy understood that his reassuring words and calming presence helped to generate more successful outcomes in the surgeries he performed. As he explains: "It wasn't part of my formal training, but it was pretty obvious that most people who come into a dentist's office are terrified. Somehow I always knew that if I could get them to relax a bit, if we made a human connection, then everything would work better."

Affectionately known to their friends as "Mental and Dental," Joan and Sandy recently celebrated their sixty-sixth wedding anniversary. Despite their gifts in the art of connection, things weren't always easy between them. But, unlike many of their friends who

separated when things got difficult, they worked through their challenges. Although I didn't realize it at the time, my parents' example
gave me a sense that growth and change were possible.

My passion for growth and change led me to study psychology
at Clark University in Worcester, Massachusetts, because it was the
place where Sigmund Freud and Carl Jung first visited when they
came to the United States and it was renowned for an excellent psychology department. Upon graduation I contemplated a career as
a psychotherapist, but in those days doctoral programs in clinical
psychology focused exclusively on pathology, and I was interested
in what we now call "positive psychology." The field of positive
psychology didn't exist yet, so I blazed my own trail.

Thanks to the creative support of Goddard College, I was able
to design my own master's degree program in Psycho-Physical
Re-education while training as a teacher of the Alexander Technique in London. My thesis became my first book, and that's how
I became an author. In 1979 I was invited to present on a five-day
leadership retreat in Switzerland for senior executives of a global
computer company. I made a great connection with the Human Resources VP and was asked to colead this program for many other
groups around the world. These early experiences provided a great
opportunity to learn about bringing people together, but my deeper
understanding of human relationships has emerged from the humbling lessons I learned from a difficult divorce and from more than
twenty years' work with a wonderfully wise psychotherapist. This
deep inner work helped me become more attuned to myself and, in
the process, more attuned to my clients. Learning to be fully present with clients allowed me to cultivate positive connections that, in
some cases, have lasted for decades. All this provides the soul impe-
tus behind this book.

Although there's always more work to do and lessons to
learn, my life is rich with beautiful, joyful relationships. I have an

abundance of loving friends, a marvelous network of clients who have become friends, a great relationship with my mom and dad, and, best of all, a fulfilling, happy marriage. The perspectives and insights in these pages are those that I apply on a daily basis to make the most of all my relationships.

Professionally, my primary emphasis has been on teaching people the mindset and skills of creative thinking. It's relatively easy to teach people how to generate new ideas. The hard part is getting support for those ideas and overcoming resistance to innovation and change. This demands skill in building relationships, and it often means managing conflict.

Many of my clients are champions of innovative change in companies, schools, and government agencies, and they seek help in overcoming resistance to new ideas. Resistance to change and innovation is to be expected. As Italian philosopher and statesman Niccolò Machiavelli (1469–1527) observed five hundred years ago: "It ought to be remembered that there is nothing more perilous… than to take the lead in the introduction of a new order of things. Because the innovator has for enemies all those who have done well under the old conditions, and lukewarm defenders in those who may do well under the new."

Whether you are championing innovation and positive change in your organization, trying to negotiate a fair deal with a collaborator, or dealing with a dispute with your spouse or child, your success and fulfillment will be a function of your ability to apply the art of connection.

Conjungere ad Solvendum

Conjungere ad solvendum is Latin for "Connect before solving." I made up this motto because, through teaching and facilitating innovative thinking for decades, I've discovered that the most powerful catalyst for inspiring creative breakthroughs and translating those breakthroughs into sustainable innovations is to guide people to *connect with one another first, before trying to solve a problem.* When people connect, when they are simpatico, on the same wavelength, attuned, in rapport, they are much better at generating and implementing new ideas.

When people really listen, when they are fully present with one another, it is, as pioneering psychotherapist Carl Rogers (1902–87) describes, "astonishing how elements which seem insoluble become soluble." Rogers adds that when genuine connection happens, "confusions which seem irremediable turn into relatively clear flowing streams."

This isn't just true in therapy. Connection facilitates creativity in all domains. When people truly listen to one another, something reliably magical happens: seemingly irremediable confusions do become clear flowing streams. This is true in a marriage, a friendship, or a professional collaboration.

The *art of connection* — creating and maintaining genuine rapport with others — is the key to building relationships, resolving conflict, and making creative dreams come true.

This book is for you, if you:

- Are an aspiring leader who wishes to cultivate the relationship-building skills necessary to translate creative visions into practical realities;
- Would like to differentiate yourself from the growing tendency toward shallow and superficial communication;
- Seek a stronger sense of connection and fulfillment in all your relationships;
- Wish to discover, and to help others discover, a deeper sense of meaning, purpose, and connection.

When it comes to learning and developing this art, we all need all the help we can get! Why?

Most people apply the communication strategies with which they were raised. If you come from a family who didn't express emotions openly and clearly, then chances are you will have a hard time expressing emotion yourself. If you were raised in an environment where anger was repressed and acted out in passive-aggressive ways, the odds are that you will do the same. Maybe you've seen the *Far Side* cartoon that depicts a huge auditorium with a large banner over the stage that says: "WELCOME! Convention of People from Nondysfunctional Families." Almost all of the seats are empty!

If people are not unconsciously mimicking the dysfunctional communication habits with which they were raised, they may be reacting against them or they may be getting their idea of how to communicate from some form of media, both of which can have problematic results. And then, of course, there's the depersonalizing effect of contemporary electronic communication. Positive models of the art of connection are rare. You've got to create your own, and this book will guide you in that process.

The Art of Connection has been incubating for decades based on insights and experiences that are fundamental to my evolving understanding of relationship building. Some of the material in this book has appeared in previous books that I have written, but it is reframed and contextualized here in a way that I hope you will experience as most useful and relevant to our present circumstances.

The seven skills we will explore are all timeless, but they are also especially timely and most essential for leaders now. Each chapter includes illustrative stories, relevant scientific research, and practical exercises to help you apply the skill. Let's begin by considering the profound role of the art of connection in supporting your health, happiness, and effectiveness as a leader.

Getting the Most from *The Art of Connection*

The Greatest Point of Leverage

In the classic comedy film *City Slickers*, Curly, the savvy, grizzled cowboy, played by the late great Jack Palance, imparts the secret of life to Mitch, the naive city slicker, played by Billy Crystal, as they ride their horses:

> CURLY: Do you know what the secret of life is? This. [He raises one finger.]
> MITCH: Your finger?
> CURLY: One thing. Just one thing. You stick to that, and everything else don't mean shit.
> MITCH: That's great.... But what is the "one thing"?
> CURLY: That's what you gotta figure out.

This book features many suggestions and practices throughout the text that I trust *will* be meaningful, and at the end of each chapter you'll find *one thing*, one action step, exercise, or practice that will help you get the most out of the skill discussed in the chapter.

This *one thing* is my best response to the question: *What's the greatest point of leverage* in applying this information now? Contemplating this powerful question helps individuals and organizations focus on the most potent specific action they can take to best advance their interests. Ultimately, as Curly notes, you've got to figure out relationship building for yourself. This closing section of each chapter is designed to help you get started in the most productive way.

References, Citations, and Recommendations

> I quote others only to better express myself.
> — MICHEL DE MONTAIGNE (1533–92), French philosopher

Michel de Montaigne may be reviled by high-school students for popularizing the essay as a literary form, but his quote about quoting is a perfect expression of my criteria for including the words and wisdom of others in this book. I use quotes when they are clever, memorable, or authoritative in support of a point that I believe is helpful for you.

> Most of the quotes on the internet are accurate.
> — THOMAS JEFFERSON

Like the line above, many of the quotations on various websites are *not* accurate, or they are misattributed, or both. For example, here's a wonderful quote that summarizes a major theme of the book:

> You cannot live for yourselves; a thousand fibers
> connect you with your fellow men,
> and along those fibers, as along sympathetic threads,
> run your actions as causes, and return to you as effects.
> — Commonly attributed to author
> HERMAN MELVILLE (1819–91), but actually said by
> the Anglican priest HENRY MELVILL (1798–1871)

All references and quotes in this book have been checked to ensure authenticity and accuracy. Many of the quotations from living authors and researchers have been verified directly with the source. When I didn't have direct access to the original source, I relied on Kristen Cashman, the brilliant managing editor of New World Library, and Garson O'Toole, a.k.a. the Quote Investigator, author of *Hemingway Didn't Say That: The Truth Behind Familiar Quotations*. Website links have been tested and were all functioning as we went to press.

The HAC Workplace

HAC stands for "high-acronym culture." Many of my corporate clients have TLAs (three-letter acronyms) for almost every policy and process. Acronyms are new words created from the first letters of a series of words and can be useful when utilized thoughtfully. They can make it easier for us to remember and serve as a password or bonding code for people who know what the letters represent. They work best when the new word created from the first letters relates to what the letters represent. For example, in Chapter 5 you'll discover that it's much easier to remember the principles for giving and receiving praise when you use the acronym PRAISE. You'll discover a liberal use of original acronyms throughout the book designed to make the material easier for you to remember and apply.

Invitation to Connect

Let's connect! I'm dedicated to helping you deepen your relationships, enrich your life, and grow as a leader. One of the skills you'll read about is how to make the exchange of feedback a natural part of your relationships. So let's make it part of ours! Please write to me directly with your feedback and follow-up questions. Twitter @MichaelJGelb or Michael@michaelgelb.com.

Overview

Here's a brief note on the focus of each chapter.

INTRODUCTION: Why *The Art of Connection* is the secret to health, happiness, longevity, and leadership.

1. EMBRACE HUMILITY: Why humility is the source of genuine strength and confidence, and how to cultivate it. How humility allows you to connect more effectively with self and others.

2. BE A GLOWWORM: How emotions are contagious, and the specific strategies to catch and spread the energy that brings out the best in yourself and others.

3. ACHIEVE THE THREE LIBERATIONS: Three simple but profound ways to shift out of the unconscious patterns that interfere with your ability to connect with yourself and others.

4. TRANSCEND FIXATIONS: How to move beyond the habits that limit your freedom to connect and respond, intelligently and effectively, to different types of people.

5. BALANCE ENERGY EXCHANGE: Simple, practical methods to monitor the balance of energy in relationships and adjust it when necessary.

6. BE A RARE LISTENER: Why real listening is so rare, and what you can do to improve, now! This is the chapter that everyone you know is waiting for you to read and apply, so that you will become a truly great listener.

7. TURN FRICTION INTO MOMENTUM: Three perspectives that will transform your approach to conflict, and the two most important skills for finding creative solutions to relationship challenges.

Introduction

The Secret of Health, Happiness, and Leadership

A leader isn't good because they are right; they are good because they listen and build trust.

— GENERAL STANLEY McCHRYSTAL, Commander, Joint Special Operations Command and U.S. Forces Afghanistan (retired)

I n April 1980, President Jimmy Carter authorized an attempt to rescue the fifty-three Americans held hostage by the Iranian Revolutionary Guards. *The Atlantic* magazine describes the result: "Everything went wrong.... America's elite rescue force lost eight men, seven helicopters, and a C-130, and had not even made contact with the enemy. It was a debacle. It defined the word 'debacle.'"

The elite Delta Force that crashed and burned in the Iranian desert was hampered by the requirement that it check with Washington before making field decisions. Its command structure was rigidly hierarchical, and its leader was frequently described as capricious, arrogant, and egotistical.

In the intensive soul searching that followed, progressive elements within the U.S. military began rethinking the traditional

21

approach to command and control and eventually developed a new operational philosophy. General Stanley McChrystal, among whose other accomplishments was the successful hunt for Abu Musab al-Zarqawi, is one of the leading proponents of this new way of thinking. McChrystal and his colleagues realized that to meet "the unrelenting demand for continual adaptability" they had to "unlearn" a great deal of what they thought they knew "about how war — and the world — worked."

They realized that the trust and alignment that characterized small operational units must be scaled up throughout the organization. They discovered that for this to happen, open, clear, and timely communication was essential. Moreover, they realized that each unit must have a deep understanding of the mission and challenges of the other units. Open, clear, and timely communication combined with empathy results in what the general calls "shared consciousness."

As the commander of a global force distributed around the world, a force made up of men and women from diverse backgrounds and largely dependent on the use of electronic communication technology, McChrystal emphasizes his most significant realization: "I learned that personal relationships are more important than ever."

Connection Is What It's All About

Brené Brown holds a PhD in social work and is a research professor at the University of Houston Graduate College of Social Work. She's a general on a different type of battlefield than McChrystal. Brown deals with humanity's inner conflicts. She explores the treacherous terrain of shame and the inner terrorism of self-doubt and feelings of worthlessness.

In her TED talk viewed by more than five million, she emphasizes the fundamental importance of the art of connection: "By the time you're a social worker for ten years...what you realize is that connection…gives purpose and meaning to our lives. This is what it's all about."

The art of connection is the key to success for soldiers and social workers, and for you. The latest research makes it clear that it's also the secret of personal happiness, health, and longevity.

Psychiatrist and professor at Harvard Medical School Robert J. Waldinger is the current director of the Laboratory of Adult Development at Massachusetts General Hospital, where he oversees the world's longest-running study of happiness. For more than seventy-seven years the lab has followed a group of 724 men, measuring the factors that most influence their mental and physical health.

Waldinger and his three predecessors all found that most younger men believe that money, power, achievement, and fame are the keys to success and happiness. That's certainly the impression one gets from contemporary media, advertising, video games, and reality television. But the results of the study are undeniably clear: the most important factor in a happy and healthy life is *a positive sense of connection with others*.

As Waldinger concludes: "The good life is built with good relationships."

His conclusions are supported and extended by many other studies. The sense of positive social connectedness yields many research-validated benefits. It:

- strengthens immune function and reduces inflammation.
- prevents dementia, diabetes, and many other ailments.
- promotes longevity.

Emma Seppälä, science director at Stanford University's Center for Compassion and Altruism Research and Education and the author of *The Happiness Track* explains, "Social connection improves physical health and mental and emotional well-being." She adds: "People who feel more connected to others have lower levels of anxiety and depression. Moreover, studies show they also have

higher self-esteem, greater empathy for others, are more trusting
and cooperative, and, as a consequence, others are more open to
trusting and cooperating with them. In other words, social connectedness generates a positive feedback loop of social, emotional, and
physical well-being."

As Seppälä suggests, positive social connectedness spreads happiness, and empathy and compassion seem to generate more of the
same. When the Dalai Lama says, "My religion is kindness," it's
more than just a sweet, offhand remark. It's an expression of ancient
wisdom that's validated by contemporary research.

E PLURIBUS UNUM

E pluribus unum, Latin for "Out of many, one," is the original motto for
the United States of America. After the tragic events of September
11, 2001, Michael Lee Stallard was inspired by the way many people
in the New York area came together as one. Shortly thereafter he
founded E Pluribus Partners, a firm dedicated to helping individuals,
organizations, and society thrive through the art of connection.

I asked Stallard, the author of *Connection Culture: The Competitive Advantage of Shared Identity, Empathy, and Understanding at
Work*, about the development of his passion. He responded that his
business training had caused him to focus on numbers and metrics,
so it took a long time to develop an appreciation for the importance of
the human element. Gradually, during his twenty-five-year tenure on
Wall Street, he noticed how morale affected performance for better or
worse. In one notable instance, a toxic culture led him to feel that his
"life force was being drained away."

After Stallard was promoted to chief marketing officer for the
global private wealth-management department of an international
brokerage firm, he realized he could put into practice the lessons he'd

learned about building positive relationships, first internally among his direct subordinates, then throughout his organization, and finally with clients and other stakeholders. The result? Revenues more than *doubled* over a two-and-a-half-year period. Stallard exults, "People were happy, and we were dramatically more profitable!"

Then a more personal challenge led him to make the art of connection the primary focus in life. He explains: "My wife, Katie, was diagnosed with breast cancer. The kindness and compassion of many of the health-care workers at our local hospital, some of whom were cancer survivors themselves, were a great comfort. Many of them went way beyond their regular duties to make a human connection with us in a way that boosted our spirits."

A year later the Stallards were confronted with more adversity when Katie was diagnosed with ovarian cancer. Her treatment included regular chemotherapy at the Memorial Sloan Kettering Cancer Center in New York. Stallard says that the professionalism and expertise of the physicians were complemented by what they experienced as a surprising level of genuine personal warmth and caring from everyone on the staff.

He notes: "One day while Katie was having a treatment, I went to the gift shop to get something to drink and stumbled on a meeting in the adjacent lounge where hospital workers were discussing an employee survey. I overheard them share that they loved working there, because they loved their colleagues, their patients, and their cause: to provide the best cancer care, anywhere!"

Katie is in remission for both cancers. Stallard is convinced that the loving-kindness they felt from everyone at the hospital and from friends and family was the key element in her recovery. Stallard experienced a life-changing epiphany as he realized the power of connection to both make his business more profitable and keep his beloved wife alive.

"Connection," he says, "is the secret of life! It gets us through the inevitable difficult seasons we all experience. It helps us grow in competence and character and makes us healthier, happier, and more productive."

The Friendship Algorithm

To be honest, I really don't give a damn about the brain.
I care about the human soul.

— MARCO IACOBONI, Director, Transcranial Magnetic Stimulation
Lab at the Ahmanson-Lovelace Brain Mapping Center, UCLA

In a 2009 episode of the sitcom *The Big Bang Theory*, Sheldon, the idiosyncratic and socially inept theoretical physicist, decides that making friends may help him get privileged access to the main computer at the university. He develops a scientific approach, constructing an algorithm to figure out the most efficient strategy to befriend the computer's gatekeeper. The result is predictably hilarious.

There's more scientific information available today about social connection and the power of relationships than ever before, and yet the general level of "people skills" seems to be declining. Indeed, there are plenty of neuroscientists who don't seem to have well-developed interpersonal intelligence.

Marco Iacoboni, author of *Mirroring People: The Science of Empathy and How We Connect with Others*, is an exception. We connected a few years ago while sharing the stage at the International Conference on Happiness and Its Causes, in Australia, featuring His Holiness the Dalai Lama. Marco's warmth, openness, and friendliness inspired me to tell him, over a bottle of spicy Aussie Shiraz, "It's a relief to know that the pioneer of mirror neuron research is a really nice guy."

I asked him to summarize his research on human nature and to comment on the dominance of the centuries-old belief that we are selfish beings, designed primarily for self-preservation.

Marco responded by telling me about his lunch with the Dalai Lama and the legendary primatologist Jane Goodall at the Australian conference, where they discussed this exact issue. He enthused: "Jane Goodall shared extraordinary stories of prosocial behavior in the animal kingdom, including examples of altruistic behavior in snakes. Snakes! How can snakes be altruistic and humans aren't?" He continued, "Our work suggests that human nature is, indeed, fundamentally prosocial, and if anything, we unlearn our natural empathy through socialization."

In other words, *we are born to be empathic.* Our brains have evolved special cells known as "mirror neurons" that attune us to others, so we can feel what they feel, instantly, reflexively, and effortlessly. Marco comments: "When I see you smile or grimace in pain, I don't have to do complex reasoning about your state of mind. I get it right away, because my brain mirrors you. This creates a powerful connection between us."

Marco explains that neuroscience is illuminating the mechanisms that make it clear that empathy can be developed. The positive implications for the amelioration of a range of mental-health challenges such as narcissistic personality disorder or autism are obvious, but there are broader implications as well. He emphasizes: "I believe it's essential for anyone in a position of leadership, and it's also important for pretty much anyone who wants better relationships. Just as athletes train themselves in their sport, you can develop your ability to connect with others. There are many ways, but if I have to find a common denominator, I'd say that focusing on the art of human connection is what is needed."

The Art in Context

General McChrystal realized that his forces had to break down the command silos and rigid hierarchy that hampered their agility. Since leading my first senior management seminar in 1979, the organizations with which I've consulted have been working to transform themselves in a manner similar to what the general recommends.

The broad megatrends involve moving from hierarchical structures to more collaborative ones, from "command and control" to an emphasis on participation and cooperation. When I started leading seminars, female participants were rare. Now more than half of my clients are women. Workplaces are far more diverse, and intrinsic incentives are increasingly important.

But many people still haven't incorporated the relationship-building skills that support evolving cultures and more flexible structures. And the challenge is growing, as we are awash in a tsunami of spam and bloated by infobesity. The skills of listening and communicating seem to be declining rapidly. Why? And what can you do about it?

Overcoming ADD

A wealth of information creates a poverty of attention.

— HERBERT SIMON (1916–2001), Nobel Laureate in Economics

I love the internet. I love connecting with friends, family, and clients anywhere, at any time, and I love having immediate access to all human knowledge. It's a dream come true. In 1982, I moved to Washington, DC, the place where creative thinking, communication, and leadership skills were, and still are, most urgently needed. I met some very interesting people, including members of a U.S. Army think tank (called the First Earth Battalion, featured many years later in the book and movie *The Men Who Stare at Goats*) who were working on a new idea called "the net," a system to allow people around the world to communicate electronically.

Five hundred years earlier, the great Italian polymath Leonardo da Vinci (1452–1519) predicted: "Men standing in opposite hemispheres will converse and deride each other and embrace each other, and understand each other's language." But even a genius like Leonardo might not have foreseen the pandemic of addiction to digital devices. Overdependence on technology is perverting our ability to develop human relationships and damaging our brains and our bodies.

At a recent CEO summit, Richard J. Davidson, professor of psychology and psychiatry at the University of Wisconsin–Madison, explained, "I think if we're all honest about it, we all suffer from attention deficit disorder, and it's in part attributable to the kind of exposure we have to digital devices." Davidson added, "Device dependence is highly reinforcing, so it becomes like a drug. And in fact it co-opts the same brain systems that are indicated in addiction." In other words, ADD (attention deficit disorder) is getting worse because of ADD (addiction to digital devices).

In addition to co-opting brain systems, addiction to digital devices causes significant debilitating effects on the body. "Text neck" and "iPosture" are some of the new terms to describe the damaging consequences of ADD. As one reporter asked in the lead to a story on this issue, "Is too much technology taking your body back to the Stone Age?" Jack Stern, a board-certified spine surgeon and author of *Ending Back Pain: 5 Powerful Steps to Diagnose, Understand, and Treat Your Ailing Back*, thinks that the answer is yes. Stern explains: "There's a pandemic of orthopedic ailments — back pain, stiff necks, frozen shoulders — caused or exacerbated by the distortion of posture associated with the use of handheld devices. It's worst among the younger generation. They're exhibiting symptoms previously associated with advanced age." In addition to orthopedic symptoms, overuse of technology also contributes to what Stern describes as a "growing sense of loneliness, alienation, and disconnection."

Device-induced discoordination results in a gradual diminishing of individual stature. As your physical stature is compromised by habitually slumping over your phone or computer, the power of your presence declines. Your stature and presence have a powerful effect, for better or worse, on your ability to focus your attention, and your ability to focus attention is an essential aspect of your experience of connection, or rapport, with others. In *Focus: The Hidden Driver of Excellence,* Daniel Goleman explains: "Rapport demands joint attention — mutual focus. Our need to make an effort to have such human moments has never been greater, given the ocean of distractions we navigate daily."

The seven relationship-building skills we will explore will help you stay afloat, ride the waves, and adjust your course to the port you desire.

ZEN KOANS FOR THE INTERNET AGE

If an anonymous comment goes unread, is it still irritating?
If nobody likes your selfie, what is the value of the self?
To see a man's true face, look to the photos he hasn't posted.
— Brandon Specktor, humorist

Look Up!

Sheryl Sandberg, COO of Facebook and author of *Lean In: Women, Work, and the Will to Lead,* reported from the World Economic Forum at Davos on a study by the global consulting firm McKinsey showing that more than 50 percent of people on Facebook have connections in other countries. Sandberg explained that these international connections are growing exponentially and wrote: "This matters. In a connected world, it's easier to...identify with people from other cultures — to understand their lives, or see things from their point of view. Technology is driving real progress in the world — raising living standards, creating new jobs and even new industries. Connectivity provides education, better health, a greater understanding of civil rights all around the world." She added, "And when people make friendships across borders, things get better for everyone."

Our electronic interconnectivity creates the framework for global shared consciousness. The key is to be wired and digitally savvy without distorting your body and losing your soul. The way to do that is not just to "lean in," but to *look up*!

How do we make the most of this amazing resource without succumbing to the detrimental aspects? Start with ART.

ART: Attention Restoration Therapy

Right now, I'm at work, using the internet. But in my mind,
I'm already at home, using the internet.
— Tweeted by BRIDGER WINEGAR @Bridger_w

Jason Hirschhorn, a super savvy Gen Xer, is the CEO and curator of Redef, a creative online platform aiming to "live at the epicenter where the worlds of media, fashion, sports, music, and tech collide." Jason asks, "Anyone know where I can find an iPad costume? I figure if I dress up like one, my nieces and nephew will look me in the eye…" Jason understands that attention is the fuel of connection. It's a precious resource, and it's being dispersed and depleted in an unprecedented way.

In *The Shallows: What the Internet Is Doing to Our Brains*, Nicholas Carr warns that the effect of overuse of the internet on our brains is "even more disturbing" than he had suspected. He notes, "The Net seizes our attention only to scatter it!"

How can we restore our capacity for the refined attention that is the currency of connection? Here are a few simple, potentially life-changing ideas.

Celebrate a digital sunset. I love wine. I usually have a glass or two with dinner. But every now and then I take the night off. If I'm served wine at a party and it isn't high quality (yes, I am a wine snob), I simply won't drink it and will have water instead. I'm blessed with a constitution that isn't prone to addiction when it comes to alcohol. It's harder for me to resist checking my iPhone than it is to say no to a generic Merlot. So I've instituted a few policies to help keep my mind free, including regular breaks during my work day and my own version of what Brian Johnson, author and founder of *A Philosopher's Notes*, describes as his "digital sunset."

Brian explains: "I turn off the computer at dinnertime and return it to its not-gonna-see-you-till-tomorrow home, appreciate all that's been done, look ahead to the next day, clean up my desk, and that's it. Time to recover." Brian adds: "My business operates online, so if I'm not careful, I could be consumed by it. Since I made the commitment to just shut it all off at the end of each workday, I have way more energy and I think with more clarity. Not to mention the improvement in my relationship with my wife and beautiful daughters."

Be in nature, and let nature be in you. The internet presents an unprecedented opportunity for connectedness and learning and an unlimited potential for distraction and dissipation. In a typical week we are exposed to more stimuli than our grandparents received in a year. In that same week, we engage with more information than our great grandparents did in their entire lives.

You can counter the effects of the information onslaught by devoting time to be in nature. Eva Selhub, author of *Your Brain on Nature*, explains: "Twenty minutes of walking in the park is an effective antidote for the symptoms of technology addiction (as long as you don't take your device along!). The research shows clearly that being in nature results in improvements in cognitive functioning, creativity, mood, and physical well-being." Selhub adds: "If you can't get to a park or other natural setting, then the next best thing is to practice a mind-body discipline like meditation, tai chi, or yoga. Like walking in nature, these disciplines all shift your nervous system from sympathetic to parasympathetic dominance, in other words from stress to relaxation."

Focus on your passion and purpose. Leonardo da Vinci advised, "Fix your course to a star." This was the Maestro's way of encouraging us to focus on our highest values and deepest purpose. It's a theme that runs throughout his life and work.

Columnist David Brooks translates Leonardo's advice in compelling contemporary terms in the *New York Times*: "If you want to win the war for attention, don't try to say no to trivial distractions you find on the information smorgasbord; try to say yes to the subject that arouses a terrifying longing, and let the terrifying longing crowd out everything else." In other words, when you are guided by higher values and embrace a deeper purpose, you'll be less distractible.

As you free yourself from ADD, you'll liberate tremendous energy that will allow you to experience the heart of the art of connection, which is to *make relationships a priority.*

The Importance of Relationships

Philosopher Martin Buber (1878–1965) observed, a century ago, that our world was becoming increasingly impersonal, materialistic, and transactional. He saw that when we view others as objects, to be manipulated or used for our own ends, we dehumanize not only them, but also ourselves. Buber emphasized that in every interaction we have a choice to view others as fellow humans, with whom we share the same basic essence, or as things — pawns to be moved, scenery for our dramas, obstacles in our way, or as competitors to be vanquished.

"I–It" is the term he originated to express the transactional, objectifying interaction. "I–Thou," from the title of his most famous work, *I and Thou* (1923), is the term he originated to refer to the encounter that creates a real connection. The most important point in this book is: Make I–Thou encounters with real people, in real time, a priority. We must invest in one-on-one, face-to-face relationships with the people who are most important to us.

If you are in a formal position of leadership, make it a priority to meet one-on-one with your team members, customers, and key stakeholders. If you are a parent, devote time to connect deeply with each of your children. If you're a friend, go out of your way to be with your friend. If you want to have a happy marriage or loving partnership, make quality time together your top priority.

Buber counseled that we come into our full aliveness, discover our true nature, and relate to the Divine through our encounters with others. He wrote, "All real life is meeting."

In addition to the emotional and spiritual benefits of deepening your ability to connect with others, you'll also be more successful. Gary Spitalnik expresses it in practical business terms when he exclaims: "I have to keep after some of the younger members of our sales team to get out from behind their desks, get the hell off their devices, and actually go out and visit with clients. That's where the real action is: face-to-face."

Jon Miller, former CEO of AOL and now a partner with Advancit Capital, says:

> I share a tremendous amount of information with my partners and our stakeholders through digital means, but there's no substitute for meeting in person. We never invest in a company without meeting the principals face-to-face. Actually

we won't consider a deal unless at least two of our three partners meet with the entrepreneurs directly, and we prefer to ensure that all three of us sit down with them personally. There's a feeling, a sense of the people, that you just can't get from reading the documents or talking on the phone. That's why I'm always flying around the country and the world. Showing up, being present, has always been important, but it's probably more important now than ever before.

THE EFFECTIVENESS OF FACE-TO-FACE COMMUNICATION

According to a study recently published in the *Journal of Experimental Social Psychology*, most people "underestimate the power of their persuasiveness in face-to-face communication," and they put too much confidence in electronic text.

Vanessa Bohns, assistant professor of organizational behavior at Cornell University and her colleague Mahdi Roghanizad discovered that a request made in person is much more likely to be fulfilled than one sent by email. Bohns found: "Despite the reach of email, asking in person is the significantly more effective approach; you need to ask six people in person to equal the power of a 200-recipient email blast." In other words, face-to-face requests were thirty-four times more likely to be fulfilled. Why is direct, interpersonal communication so much more impactful? Bohns discovered that subtle, nonverbal clues "made all the difference" in the relative power of the face-to-face interactions.

She concludes, "If your office runs on email and text-based communication, it's worth considering whether you could be a more effective communicator by having conversations in person."

Direct, face-to-face connections aren't just the secret of individual professional success; they're the cornerstone of great businesses. In the groundbreaking classic *Firms of Endearment: How World-Class Companies Profit from Passion and Purpose*, Babson Business School professor Raj Sisodia and his coauthors, Jag Sheth, and David Wolfe, make it clear that today's greatest organizations succeed by helping *all* their stakeholders thrive: customers, investors, employees, partners, communities, and society. They make the world better by the way they do business, and the world responds by making them more profitable. This isn't touchy-feely idealism; it's practical, evidence-based reality. The firms studied by Sisodia and his colleagues have outperformed the Standard & Poor's 500 by fourteen times and the companies featured in Jim Collins's bestseller *Good to Great* by six times over a period of fifteen years.

The research presented in *Firms of Endearment* illuminates "radical new rules" for building an intentional, profitable, high-performance business. Among those new rules, this one is fundamental: "Create partner relationships that really are mutually beneficial." The I–Thou encounter is the secret that brings this rule to life.

Connecting with Ourselves

We create ourselves through connection with others, and we deepen our capacity to connect with others through the work we do to connect with ourselves.

Leonardo da Vinci loved to contemplate the ripples that radiate out when a stone is tossed into a still pond. He wrote, "Everything is connected to everything else." What if your posts on social media, your everyday conversations, your internal dialogue about the state of the world all rippled out to enliven — or dull — the consciousness of others? In the Buddhist scriptures, the *Avatamsaka Sutra* presents an image of this interconnected consciousness known as the Jewel Net of Indra.

Here's my interpretation of what it says. Imagine that the cosmos is structured as an infinite net, a multidimensional spider web, stretching to eternity in all directions. At every intersection of the gossamer strands is a perfect glittering diamond star. The diamond stars are infinite in number, and each one reflects the radiance of all the others. In the metaphor of Indra's Net each of us is a jewel linked to, and reflecting, all the other jewels.

We are all precious jewels. Our mirror neurons reflect the many facets of consciousness. How can we polish the mirror to better illuminate our true nature and our interconnectedness? And how can we translate that illumination into better relationships, a more intelligent approach to conflict, and greater effectiveness in achieving our goals together?

We begin with a process of self-observation and reflection. If you bring your attention right now to your bodily sensations, feelings, and thoughts, it's obvious that there's a fundamental aspect of you that isn't your body, emotions, or thoughts. This is your consciousness, your self-awareness.

The key to polishing your mirror is becoming more aware of the habits of body, feeling, and thought that interfere with your ability to be fully present and learning to let them go. As you let go of the unnecessary, clarity emerges. As clarity emerges, you experience a deeper sense of connection.

About the fact that our ability to connect with others is predicated on our connection with ourselves, psychologist and philosopher Rollo May (1909–94) has this to say:

> Finding the center of strength within ourselves is in the long run the best contribution we can make to our fellow men.... One person with indigenous inner strength exercises a great calming effect on panic among people around him. This is what our society needs — not new ideas and inventions, important as these are, and not geniuses and supermen, but

persons who can *be*, that is, persons who have a center of strength within themselves.

Beyond the obvious intrinsic value of the process of aligning with this center of strength, our commitment to the process of growth and change, as May suggests, has a powerful effect on others. Business guru Peter Drucker observed that in the workplace a leader "who works on his own development sets an almost irresistible example."

The example you set and the influence you have by working on your own development and reflecting on questions pertaining to your self-knowledge may be even more important in parenting and partnership than they are professionally.

Irish playwright Oscar Wilde (1854–1900) quipped, "Only the shallow know themselves." He's right. Genuine self-knowledge isn't a static state, but rather a continuous quest, a never-ending journey.

The Seven Relationship-Building Skills

I thought we were going to be together forever.
Then right out of the blue she sends me a "John Deere" letter…
something about me not listening enough. I don't know…
I wasn't really paying attention.
— From the film *DUMB AND DUMBER*

Positive relationships are fundamental to leadership and business success. But as Daniel Goleman, author of *Emotional Intelligence* observes: "Western business people often don't get the importance of establishing human relationships."

Although individuals from many other cultures put relationships first, in the United States there's still a tendency to focus more on the transaction than the connection. In many professions we are initiated into the use of various kinds of jargon, codes, and insider acronyms without necessarily learning how to genuinely connect with others. Whatever the field — information technology, biochemistry, engineering, psychology — there's an increasing tendency for people to speak in a language understood only by their immediate professional tribe. A partner from a Washington, DC, law firm once told me his wife complained that he always spoke to her like a lawyer. When I asked him how he responded, he replied, "I requested that she present the evidence behind that assertion."

In a recent seminar for a New York–based construction management company, we were exploring the role of the art of connection in the functioning of the company's safety effort, in marketing its services, and in its ability to manage huge construction projects — coordinating the efforts of carpenters, electricians, and architects in the midst of other workers pouring concrete and operating giant cranes in the crowded Manhattan landscape. As the seminar participants contemplated the key to success in all these endeavors, it became clear that the quality of communication was the most important element in their work. One of the participants experienced this as an epiphany. He exclaimed, "Oh my God. I get it! We're not in the construction business — we're in the relationship business."

We are *all* in the relationship business! Now, leaders who cultivate the art of connection will have an increasingly powerful advantage over those who don't.

1

Embrace Humility

Do you wish to rise? Begin by descending. You plan a tower that will pierce the clouds? Lay first the foundation of humility.

— ST. AUGUSTINE (354–430), author of *The City of God*

E ven before the advent of the internet, "communication" was the number-one problem identified in surveys of organizational challenges. It's usually at the top of most lists of personal challenges as well. Let's begin with a simple exercise that illuminates the problem.

Word-Association Exercise

Please get a piece of blank paper and a pen or use your computer or digital device to make a list numbered 1 to 10. In a moment you'll get a word to write at the top of the list.

As soon as you've written that word, please write the first ten words you think of related to the word at the top. Put down your first ten associations with that top word as quickly as you can, without judging or editing. In a word-association exercise there are no wrong answers.

Ready? The word is: *art*.

After you complete your ten word associations, consider the associations that might have been written for the same word by one of your peers, your spouse, your best friend, or your boss. How many words would you have in common with that person? Most people are surprised to discover the differences that appear when they compare their results with others'. It's rare for a group to have much in common at all.

In one group, for example, Jane's first word was *Warhol*, the name of her favorite visual artist. Jim's first association was *Garfunkel*, a singer whose first name is Art. Dinah wrote *martial*, as she had just begun studying martial arts, while Roger, an aspiring poet, wrote *heart* and nine other rhyming words. The group was surprised to discover just how different their associations were.

When a group of accountants did this exercise with similar results, they became very upset. They prided themselves on their uniformity and felt that the diversity of their responses to the word mocked their standardized procedures. In their words, "We're not artists; we're accountants." They insisted that they be given a word that had something to do with their work and that they would then produce greater commonality. When they were given the word *money*, however, they had even less in common.

Occasionally, people do get one or two words in common, but when you explore the results further and ask them to associate ten words with the shared word, you find that they usually meant something different by the common word after all.

The Paradox Every Leader Needs to Understand

Our associations are unique. Even if we belong to a group classified in some way — accountants, artists, teachers, carpenters, secretaries, doctors, lawyers, or Cajun chefs — each of us is an individual. Each of us, as a result of heredity combined with individual experience, construes the world in our own unique way. We each are gifted with a special ability to experience and express the wonder of being alive. There is no one else like you, no one who can think and create exactly as you do.

This diversity is an important expression of the evolutionary process that helps ensure the survival of the species. Given any type of adverse circumstance that may befall humanity, there is probably someone with the special ability to overcome the challenge.

According to the Population Research Bureau (PRB), approximately 108 billion humans have populated the planet since the advent of the species. Each person who has come and gone was unique, and each of the 7.5 billion people alive today is unique. There's no one like you in all of human history. The combination of your genetic endowment and the way that genetic material is influenced by your life experience results in a one-of-a-kind phenomenon.

And yet, in so many ways, we are all the same. Our basic human needs — for air, food, shelter, security, esteem, love, and so on — are universal. Everyone, everywhere, in every culture wants respect. Leadership is the art of skillfully meeting universal human needs, including the need to be appreciated for being unique and the need for a sense of belongingness and connection.

UNIQUENESS AND BELONGINGNESS

Jeanine Prime and Elizabeth Salib, of the Catalyst Research Center for Advancing Leader Effectiveness, highlight an important paradox: "Our research was also able to isolate the combination of two separate, underlying sentiments that make employees feel included: uniqueness *and* belongingness. Employees feel unique when they are recognized for the distinct talents and skills they bring to their teams; they feel they belong when they share important commonalities with coworkers."

Prime and Salib add: "It's tricky for leaders to get this balance right, and emphasizing uniqueness too much can diminish employees' sense of belonging. However, we found that altruism is one of the key attributes of leaders who can coax this balance out of their employees, almost across the board."

An Art of Infinite Possibility

Our associations are unique, and they are potentially unlimited. Our minds are capable of linking any thought with any other thought. If you doubt this, try to find a word that cannot be linked to the word *art*. No matter how hard you search for an unrelatable word, you'll discover that your mind can connect anything to anything else.

The exercise of finding unrelatable words is particularly fun when framed as a competition. For example, when a group of biochemists were challenged to think of a word that "could not, in any way, be related to *art*," one clever PhD suggested that *antidisestablishmentarianism* couldn't be linked to *art*. But another erudite member of the group pointed out that the word means "opposition to the disestablishment of orthodox churches," which opposed, among other things, the practice of many popular arts. Someone else mentioned that the word *antidisestablishmentarianism* actually contains the letters of the word for *art*. Another person explained that you can automatically connect this or any other strange word with *art* as a member of that class of words you don't normally associate with *art*.

Your mind can connect anything with anything else and can make a potentially infinite number of connections with any word you hear or read, but your way of associating, of making connections, is unique. This is good news if you are interested in creative thinking. If every individual has the capacity to generate unlimited associations, and each person has a unique way of doing it, then every group possesses vast potential for ideation.

When it comes to the art of connection, however, the implications are daunting, as the potential for *misunderstanding* in any communication is also unlimited. My mind is capable of making an unlimited number of associations with every single word that you say, and if your way of saying things and my way of hearing things is unique to each of us, it begins to seem amazing that we can communicate at all.

When we depend on words primarily, misunderstanding is to be expected. One reason that relationships seem to be degrading is that many people rely increasingly on text and email as their means of relating with others. But emoticons do not serve as effective substitutes for the body language, voice tonality, and eye contact that help us understand the context and meaning of words.

Even with the benefit of context, misunderstanding is pandemic. How many times have you had the experience of carefully explaining something to someone, watching him nod in apparent understanding, and seeing him do something entirely different from what you thought you'd agreed upon?

The Telephone Game

Much of our communication is reminiscent of the children's game Telephone, which was a popular party activity when I was a child. I didn't imagine then that I would employ it with groups of corporate executives many years later and that it would be a hilarious and memorable team-building activity that also illuminates a fundamental difficulty in communication.

The game works best with a group of eight or more people. It begins when the facilitator whispers a phrase into the ear of the first player, who then turns and whispers it into the ear of the next person, and so on. (The whisper should be soft enough so that only the intended recipient can hear the message.) After the message goes around, the last person to receive it states the message aloud. Invariably, the original phrase goes through so much distortion in the process of sharing that the final product is not only different from the original, but often hilariously so.

For example, in a recent session, a group of twelve bankers managed to turn "Robots randomly write regulatory rulebooks" into "Blue bots rewrite regular glory books on domes." The game is amusing and highlights the extent to which our communication is subject to radical misunderstanding.

THE ILLUSION OF TRANSPARENCY

If you tapped out a familiar song like "Happy Birthday" or the national anthem on a table or even directly on a friend's arm, how likely do you think it is that your friend can guess the tune you are tapping? In a dissertation entitled "Overconfidence in the Communication of Intent: Heard and Unheard Melodies," Elizabeth Newton found that subjects believed that the song they tapped would be guessed correctly by their partners about half the time, but the study showed that the tune was guessed accurately in only 3 percent of trials.

Psychologists call this phenomenon the *illusion of transparency*. Since we think we know what we mean when we say something, we tend to imagine that it's clear to others as well. But just as most people can't decode the tune you tap for them, our potential for clear communication remains untapped when we assume that others understand what we intend to communicate.

The Grand Illusion

I know that you believe that you understood
what you think I said, but I am not sure you realize
that what you heard is not what I meant.
— ROBERT MCCLOSKEY,
former U.S. State Department spokesman

What's the single greatest problem in communication? *The illusion
that it has taken place successfully!* The illusion is pandemic. Misunderstanding, predicated on inaccurate assumptions, is the default
setting in human relationships.

Instead of assuming that you have effectively understood someone else or been understood yourself, you can minimize misunderstanding and build relationships more effectively by embracing
humility.

Humility Is the Soul of Leadership

I stand here before you not as a prophet,
but as a humble servant of you, the people.
— NELSON MANDELA (1918–2013), former president of
South Africa, on February 11, 1990, the day of his release
after twenty-seven years of imprisonment

If you are humble, then you will be more curious and open to learning the art of connection. You will be poised to enrich your life by
building better relationships.

Humility is the catalyst of curiosity. Curiosity is the driver of
continuous learning. Continuous learning is the key to developing
the relationship-building skills every leader needs now. Give up assuming that you know what others are thinking and feeling. Assume
that you don't know and become curious to learn.

In a recent *Harvard Business Review* article, Jeanine Prime and Elizabeth Salib explain why today's best leaders have to be humble: "In a global marketplace where problems are increasingly complex, no *one* person will ever have all the answers." Reporting on a study of more than fifteen hundred global associates of multinational companies, they conclude that humility is a critical leadership factor and that it is especially important "for creating an environment where employees from different demographic backgrounds feel included."

What are the specific behaviors associated with being perceived as a humble leader? The key elements include:

- encouraging dialogue instead of debate
- modeling curiosity by asking questions
- welcoming feedback

Prime and Salib conclude: "When leaders showcase their own personal growth, they legitimize the growth and learning of others; by admitting to their own imperfections, they make it okay for others to be fallible, too."

Bill George, former CEO of Medtronic, a professor at Harvard Business School, and the author of *Discover Your True North*, agrees. He writes, "The finest leaders are keenly aware of their limitations and the importance of teams around them in creating their success." George confesses that early in his career he wasn't humble and admits that his insecurities drove him to act as though he was invulnerable and that he could solve any problem independently.

As he matured, he realized that humility allowed him to connect more effectively with others and thereby to bring out the best in the people he led. He explains:

> As my inner confidence grew, I no longer needed to have all the answers or try to impress others with what I had done. I freely admitted my mistakes and learned that doing so enabled others to acknowledge their errors. I recognized vulnerability is power....As I did so, people gained greater

confidence in my leadership and expressed increased desire to join me in common pursuits.

HUMILITY IS A COMPETITIVE ADVANTAGE

In a report entitled "Expressed Humility in Organizations: Implications for Performance, Teams, and Leadership," Bradley Owens and his colleagues emphasize that humility is more than just a virtue; it's a critical key to high performance and effective leadership. Their studies reveal that humble leaders are more effective at facilitating employee engagement and encouraging a collaborative approach to learning.

The research team defined *humility* as "an interpersonal characteristic that emerges in social contexts that connotes (a) a manifested willingness to view oneself accurately, (b) a displayed appreciation of others' strengths and contributions, and (c) teachability." They developed a method to measure this characteristic and then utilized it to predict academic and job performance.

Previous research showed that diligence and intelligence were the best indicators of performance. But the surprising result of this study was that humility was an even better predictor.

If humility comes naturally to you, then you have an advantage. If it doesn't, however, there's no need to despair, as the researchers also report that it's a quality you can cultivate. As the Foster School blog concludes, cultivating humility "might just make us more effective at school, at play, and in the workplace."

Is Vulnerability Weakness or Power?

In a seminar for construction managers, the group engaged in a discussion about the importance of seeking input from work crews on job sites. Joe, a veteran senior project manager, asked, "Won't my people think I'm weak if I ask for their ideas?" This led to a passionate discussion in which many of the younger participants shared their belief that when a boss asks for their contributions, they feel respected and included. As a result, they see this as a sign of strength.

As the discussion continued, it also became clear that, although the more junior members of the group preferred it when their suggestions were acted upon, the most important point was that they felt acknowledged. As one assistant supervisor expressed it: "It is so much better when the line of communication is open, and I feel that I'm being listened to, that someone actually gives a shit."

In the old days of top-down hierarchy, Joe's concern about asking and listening may have been well founded, but that world is fading. Now being open to the influence of others is a key to expanding your influence. American educator and author Stephen R. Covey (1932–2012) emphasizes: "You become vulnerable. It's a paradox... because in order to have influence, you have to be influenced."

In her book *Daring Greatly: How the Courage to Be Vulnerable Transforms the Way We Live, Love, Parent, and Lead*, Brené Brown argues that "vulnerability is the core, the heart, the center, of meaningful human experiences." She refers to vulnerability as the birthplace of creativity, innovation, and change.

CEO of the Charles Schwab Corporation, Walt Bettinger, adds that a leader's real power comes from touching people's hearts and that his growth as a leader demanded that he develop qualities that initially seemed "completely unnatural." As he told the *New York Times*, "It requires transparency, authenticity, vulnerability."

Vulnerable is derived from the Latin *vulnerare*, "to wound." Synonyms for *vulnerable* include *weak, helpless, defenseless, sitting duck*, and *sucker*. Bettinger and Brown aren't suggesting that you be a sucker or a sitting duck. Vulnerability isn't timidity or weakness.

Rather, it's an acknowledgment that we are sensitive, alive, and affected emotionally by our interactions and experiences.

More helpful words to express this quality include:

Accessible
Available
Approachable
Open
Present
Receptive
Responsive
Unarmored

When we are open and accessible, we are able to connect with ourselves, and we make it much easier for others to connect with us.

I learned this lesson years ago, and it was a turning point in my life both personally and professionally. When I was thirty, my career was blossoming. I'd learned how to say wise words and make a positive impression on clients, but my life, especially in the area of intimate relationships, was reflecting the need for personal growth. Although I'd done considerable work on my mind and body, my emotional center hadn't received the same amount of attention. This discrepancy seemed to be playing out in a series of less than fulfilling relationships. After rationalizing that I just hadn't met the right person, I began to consider my own responsibility and asked: "How can *I* become the right person?"

On the recommendation of a friend whose advice I heeded due to the searing accuracy of her critical feedback, I went to see a psychotherapist. This was a stretch since, having been raised by a therapist, going to therapy as a child, and studying psychology for years both academically and practically, I was skeptical, and probably arrogant, about the prospect of finding someone I'd respect.

The minute I walked into Dr. Mort Herskowitz's office, my skepticism and arrogance vanished. There was something about his penetrating gaze, purity of attention, and ease within himself that made it clear, as soon as he looked at me, that I couldn't fool him, and I soon discovered that in his presence I couldn't fool myself. He wasn't interested in anything that wasn't authentic. Mort was an uncompromising mirror of the self.

An osteopathic physician and psychiatrist, Mort trained for nine years with Wilhelm Reich (1897–1957), the legendary pioneer of depth psychology. I had studied Reich's theory of character armor, the idea that our stresses and traumas stay locked in our muscles and viscera, but believed I had sorted all that out through years of various mind and body practices. Wrong!

I worked with Mort for the better part of the next twenty years, during which time he helped me surface and fully experience the anxiety, fear, shame, and anger that I didn't even know I had. Where did all this originate? Perhaps it was inherited? Or maybe it came from unresolved childhood frustrations? I don't know. The work with Mort didn't focus on analyzing or understanding the causes; rather, it was about releasing the armor and experiencing more openness and aliveness. As difficult as this was — and it's probably the most difficult work I've ever done — it was liberating.

As I learned to breathe through the armoring, energy began moving through me in a new way, like water flowing through a fire hose when the kinks are removed. Although I experienced emotions that were far from pleasant, I invariably left Mort's office with a sense of greater connectedness to myself, the people in my life, and all of creation. The leaves of the trees on his Philadelphia street corner always looked greener and the light outside always seemed brighter when I left his office. And when the dark and frightening feelings were brought to light, they subsided and were replaced by waves of joy, gratitude, and appreciation. I started seeing Mort in the days before cell phones and email, but on the corner opposite his office was a pay phone. After each session I'd find myself picking up that phone and calling someone in my life to say, "I love you." This wasn't the expression of a superficial sentimentality, but rather an experience, at the core of my being, that loving connection is the underpinning of life.

Wilhelm Reich, Mort's teacher, wrote, "The armored, mechanistically rigid person thinks mechanistically, produces mechanistic tools, and forms a mechanistic conception of nature." In our complex and often crazy world we may feel the need to armor ourselves against the onslaught of noxious stimuli. The danger is that, as Reich warned, the armoring becomes our default setting, blocking our ability to connect with ourselves and others in a genuine way.

Working with Mort, I discovered a profound paradox. When I released my armoring and felt most open and accessible, I discovered the source of inner confidence and connection. Vulnerability is power, because being open and accessible makes real connection possible. You can work on this in therapy for decades or practice it in your everyday interactions.

CAVEAT: "TAKE CARE THAT YOUR VIRTUES BE GENUINE"

Don't be so humble. You're not that great.
— GOLDA MEIR (1898–1978), legendary Israeli prime minister,
to one of her government ministers who had made a cloyingly
inauthentic attempt at a self-deprecating remark

There is an affected humility more insufferable than downright pride,
as hypocrisy is more abominable than libertinism.
Take care that your virtues be genuine.
— ARTHUR MARTINE (ca. 1840–1902),
arbiter of etiquette, on fake humility

Develop the Common Touch

A person who is nice to you but rude to the waiter
is not a nice person.
— DAVE BARRY, humorist

One day I took a break from writing this book and went to the gro-
cery store. At checkout, I placed my romaine lettuce, pears, cheeses,
eggs, olives, and artichoke hearts on the conveyor belt, and when
the person before me finished paying, I eased forward and slid my
credit card in the machine. I looked up at the cashier anticipating
a greeting. He averted his eyes. I was surprised that he didn't ask
me the usual questions: "How are you today?" and, "Did you find
everything okay?"

I felt a chill, and a sense of alienation. Then I thought: "Hey, I'm
writing this book on the art of connection, and I've just written all
these notes about accessibility and openness. Maybe there's a way
to connect with this guy who looks like he might be having a rough
day."

During this inner dialogue, I noticed the prominent display of
an impulse item next to the register — a snack bar made of bison,
cranberries, and bacon. This seemed laughably disgusting to me,
and I wondered what the cashier thought. So I decided, on impulse,
to risk connecting. I asked him, "Do people really buy this? Have
you tried it?"

"The flavors are actually pretty decent," he said, still looking
rather grim, "but the texture is disgusting!"

We both cracked up laughing as we exchanged a gleeful glance.
I hope it brightened his day. I know it brightened mine.

Practicing the art of connection in such small, seemingly insig-
nificant everyday actions is the key to being able to utilize it when
you're confronting a challenge with someone at work or a crisis in
any relationship. As you explore building rapport with cashiers,

waiters, and others, you'll be setting the stage for greater skill in building the relationships that matter the most, whether in business or at home. If you're a cashier, you'll strengthen your immune system and elevate your mood through making positive connections with customers. If you're a waiter, you'll do more than raise oxytocin levels; you'll also receive bigger tips.

Psychologist Leo Buscaglia (1924–98), known affectionately as Dr. Love, was devoted to helping others focus on what really matters in life. He commented on the power of seemingly minor everyday interactions: "Too often we underestimate the power of a touch, a smile, a kind word, a listening ear, an honest compliment, or the smallest act of caring, all of which have the potential to turn a life around." Imagine the goodwill, engagement, and brand loyalty generated by an organization that harnesses this power.

HQCS: A LEADERSHIP SECRET FOR MANAGING ENERGY

The launch party for Arianna Huffington's Thrive Global in downtown New York City was a madhouse! Thumping loud music, way too many people jostling around in the space, massive sensory overload. In the midst of the craziness, I was introduced to Abby Levy, the CEO of Thrive. Abby did something that transformed my experience of the evening: for the twenty seconds we spoke she gave me her full attention. (And she generously offered a private tour at a quieter time.) In a graceful and efficient way, she recognized my existence. It was a moment of I-Thou.

These brief moments, like my interaction with the cashier, can make a surprising difference in the quality of our lives and our effectiveness as leaders, according to Jane Dutton, professor of business administration and psychology at the University of Michigan Ross

School of Business and coauthor of *How to Be a Positive Leader: Small Actions, Big Impact.* After studying the phenomenon of successful leadership for decades, Dutton concludes, "Leaders can bring out the best in themselves and others through high-quality connections (HQCs)."

How do you know you've had an HQC? Dutton invites us to consider:

> Think of the last time an interaction at work literally lit you up. Before the interaction, you may have felt depleted, tired, or simply neutral. After the interaction, even if it was brief, you had a greater energy and capability for action. This sense of heightened energy is real, and it is an important indicator that you are engaged in a high-quality connection.

Dutton and her colleagues make a compelling, evidence-based case for the benefits of HQCs. They've shown that people who have more high-quality connections:

- are physically and psychologically healthier.
- display greater cognitive functioning and broader capabilities for thinking.
- are more open to learning.
- are more creative and engaged at work.

For organizations, the implications are profound. Dutton explains that HQCs promote "organizational effectiveness in terms of greater efficiency and higher-quality performance." She adds, "The beauty of high-quality connections is they do not require significant time to build, because they can be created in the moment."

Adopt an HQC Mindset

In 1982, author Anne Herbert jotted down the phrase "Practice random acts of kindness and senseless acts of beauty" in a creative reinterpretation designed as an antidote to media reports of "random acts of violence and senseless acts of cruelty." Herbert's musing led to a book entitled *Random Kindness and Senseless Acts of Beauty* and innumerable bumper stickers, T-shirts, and graffiti.

One of the simplest ways to practice the art of connection is to look for opportunities to perform acts of intentional, deliberate connection and kindness in daily life. Smile and make eye contact with the teller at the bank and the clerk at the pharmacy. Hold a door open, slow down to allow another driver to enter your lane, offer your seat on a crowded subway, help someone get carry-on luggage down from the overhead bin. Notice how you feel when you do these simple acts. You'll delight others, but you'll also find that you feel better, more energized and connected.

ON HIGH-QUALITY CONNECTIONS

Positive emotions compound quickly, and these short-term
meaningful interactions stay in people's minds. It may be as brief
as looking at each other with mutual positive regard.
— JANE DUTTON and MONICA WORLINE,
Awakening Compassion at Work:
The Quiet Power That Elevates People and Organizations

All Souls Are Created Equal

When I was in my twenties and just starting out in my career in London, I was invited to tea by the CEO of a large mining company at the fabled East India Club in St. James Square. I'd never been to a British gentlemen's club before and was concerned about the proper etiquette, so I consulted my friend Yogesh, an immigrant from Mumbai who was an expert in all things British. Yogesh's most important advice, which he shared in his flawless Oxford English, was: "Whatever you do, do not thank the servants."

What a perfect evocation of the hierarchical, stratified world of the British Raj! Mahatma Gandhi (1869–1948), the catalyst of the demise of the Raj, offered very different counsel when he was the editor of a magazine in South Africa and a woman wrote to him to ask advice on assessing the character of the fiancé her parents had arranged for her. Gandhi suggested that rather than focusing on his treatment of her, she would learn much more if she observed the way he treated his servants.

Over the years I've worked closely with a number of people as they rose through the ranks of large organizations, and a number of these individuals became CEOs. All of them, without exception, are generous, kind, and considerate toward people at all levels. They all have what Nobel Laureate Rudyard Kipling (1865–1936), in his poetic meditation on what it means to be a self-actualized human, called "the common touch":

> If you can talk with crowds and keep your virtue,
> Or walk with Kings — nor lose the common touch...

In a 2016 interview, Schwab CEO Walt Bettinger describes the most important lesson he learned in business school. It came through a final exam for which he had prepared diligently, in the hope of maintaining his perfect 4.0 grade average, by memorizing formulas and details of case studies. Bettinger was surprised when he was handed just one blank piece of paper the top of which read: "I've taught you everything I can teach you about business in the last ten weeks, but the most important message, the most important question, is this: What's the name of the lady who cleans this building?" Bettinger explains: "It was the only test I ever failed....Her name was Dottie, and I didn't know Dottie. I'd seen her, but I'd never taken the time to ask her name. And that had a powerful impact.... I've tried to know every Dottie I've worked with ever since. It was just a great reminder of what really matters in life."

A MASTER OF THE COMMON TOUCH: "YOU ARE ONE OF US."

Jack Meyer, affectionately known as "Bear," is a successful Santa Fe–based art dealer, real-estate investor, accomplished chef, and all-around legendary character. A master storyteller, he seems to know everyone, everywhere, and shares spellbinding stories to match any occasion. But he offers much more than just talk.

Do you need tickets to a show that is sold out? Need an appraisal for a painting you inherited from your grandmother? Need to raise money for your start-up business? Would you like to meet the coolest people at Burning Man? Need help negotiating a deal that will result in benefits for all parties? Bear can help.

Many years ago he was an entrepreneur in the global cannabis trade, championing the mind-altering and healing properties of the then contraband substance. He transitioned to other means of support after a short stay in prison. The prescribed sentence for his offense was more than twenty years, but he charmed the court into extreme lenience. In prison, he organized and prepared home-cooked meals and served as the unofficial facilitator of a support group to help prepare his fellow inmates for life outside.

Despite his exceptional ability to adapt and adjust by making connections "inside," Jack's confinement led him to suffer from PTSD. He laughs exuberantly as he explains that the physician who treated him upon his release prescribed what scientific evidence suggests as the ideal remedy for his condition: medical marijuana.

Jack is gifted at the art of connection, and I wanted to know his secrets. He explained that his natural attunement to others was deepened by surviving abuse as a child and multiple near-death experiences. He says emphatically, "I should have been dead a number of times. I mean really dead. It's miraculous that I'm alive. And that gives me an overflowing sense of gratitude and wanting to be of service to others." He adds, "I view all people as family and see our connection to each other and all things."

His enthusiasm for people makes it possible for him to move with ease in many different worlds. One of those worlds is Duck Lake on the Blackfeet Reservation in Montana, where he takes his family on an annual fishing trip. Every year upon arrival he visits the run-down trailer on the reservation where some older folks issue permits and sell worms and other necessary gear.

He explains: "Year after year, each day of every trip, I would stop by the trailer and say hello, ask about their families and what it was like for them living on a reservation. Over the years they explained to me that they had been moved from their traditional lands and forced to give up their traditional hunter-gatherer ways to become farmers. I wondered how they felt about this. Many discussions ensued in which I learned that they had all been punished for speaking in their native tongue and their children were taken from them and sent to reservation schools."

He continues: "One year we arrived and came to the trailer to say hello and get our permits and gear. The leader of the group said, 'We have been watching you for years, and you are not like the other tourists. Would you like to stop by our house and have some coffee?'"

Jack and his wife didn't drink coffee, but they accepted the invitation and soon discovered that these were the elders of the Blackfeet Tribal Council. In the course of the many deep and lively conversations that followed, Jack and his wife were offered the privilege of purchasing a magnificent cabin on Duck Lake.

> Overjoyed and humbled by this phenomenal opportunity, Jack asked, "Why are you so nice to me?"
> They responded, "Because you are one of us."
> He protested, "But I'm a Jewish guy from Brooklyn."
> They responded, "We know you. We are sure you have Blackfeet blood. You are one of us. And now you have a Blackfeet name: Bear."

What really matters in life is connection. Gandhi, Abby, Walt, and Bear all share the attitude expressed by physicist Albert Einstein (1879–1955) when he said, "I speak to everyone in the same way, whether he is the garbage man or the president of the university." Why did Einstein speak to everyone in the same way? He believed that all life was interconnected and that our sense of separateness and ego was "a kind of optical delusion of consciousness."

The common touch isn't a form of condescension in which a higher-status person deigns to recognize, for a moment, the validity of the existence of a lower-status person. Rather, it is a recognition that everyone, whatever their status, has a soul and, to paraphrase our third president, Thomas Jefferson (1743–1826), "All souls are created equal."

When we embrace humility and curiosity, we release egotism and arrogance. We open to our own soul, and in the process we are more open to others. People sense this and become more open to us. Leaders need this skill now more than ever.

The Greatest Point of Leverage

CULTIVATE THE ART OF CONVERSATION.

In a world where children are developing their notion of conversation through interactions with Siri and Alexa, the art of direct face-to-face, eye-to-eye communication is, according to Sherry Turkle, professor of the Social Studies of Science and Technology at the Massachusetts Institute of Technology and the author of *Reclaiming Conversation: The Power of Talk in the Digital Age*, "the most human and humanizing thing that we do; it's where we learn to put ourselves in the place of the other."

Turkle champions the art of conversation as the means to awaken empathy, build all kinds of relationships, and develop your skill as a leader. Her research demonstrates that overdependence on digital devices seems to be degrading skills in this essential competency. She explains: "We haven't stopped talking, but we opt out, often unconsciously, of the kind of conversation that requires full attention. Every time you check your phone in company, what you gain is a hit of stimulation, a neurochemical shot, and what you lose is what a friend, teacher, parent, lover, or coworker just said, meant, felt."

Turkle advocates an open, curious, and free-flowing approach to connecting with others, recommending "conversations without agenda, where you discover things as you go along." When you look for something interesting and enlivening in other people, you are much more likely to find it. As Dale Carnegie advises, the way to be interesting is to be interested. Ask questions, and then ask follow-up questions and listen deeply.

The greatest point of leverage for embracing humility is to *engage in at least one real conversation with another human being every day.*

What are the keys to cultivating the art of conversation? Arthur Martine's *Hand-book of Etiquette, and Guide to True Politeness* (1866) is an all-time classic guide to conversation. Here's an imaginary conversation about conversation with direct quotes from Martine's book in italics:

Q: What's the purpose of conversation?

A: Connection, *pleasure, and improvement.*

Q: How do you know if you've had a good conversation?

A: All parties have more energy than when you began. *He who goes out of your company pleased with himself is sure to be pleased with you.*

Q: What's the best attitude to bring to a conversation?

A: Curiosity! The desire to discover something unique, interesting, or even amazing about others. And *cheerfulness, unaffected cheerfulness, a sincere desire to please and be pleased...a light and airy equanimity of temper...a feeling heart and generous mind.*

Q: How can I avoid being boring?

A: *Practice genuine humility and avoid arrogance.* Don't promote or pontificate; instead, ask open-ended questions and then ask follow-up questions.

Q: What are the appropriate subjects for conversation?

A: Subjects *only of universal interest can be made legitimate topics of pleasantry or discussion.*

Q: So we agree on the importance of looking for the soulfulness in everyone we meet, yet isn't it also important to be selective about the people with whom we choose to engage?

A: *If you have been once in company with an idle person, it is enough. You need never go again. You have heard all he knows. For idle people make no improvements. Don't give your time to every superficial acquaintance.*

Q: Would you say that the art of conversation is more about eliciting other people's enthusiasms than displaying your own wit?

A: Yes. *The great charm of conversation consists less in the display of one's own wit and intelligence than in the power to draw forth the resources of others; he who leaves you after a long conversation, pleased with himself and the part he has taken in the discourse, will be your warmest admirer.*

Q: We've discussed the importance of the common touch. What do you have to say about it?

A: *Think like the wise; but talk like ordinary people. Put yourself on the same level as the person to whom you speak, and under penalty of being considered a pedantic idiot, refrain from explaining any expression or word that you may use.*

2

Be a Glowworm

We are all worms. But I do believe I am a glowworm.

— WINSTON CHURCHILL (1874–1965), British statesman and
Nobel Laureate in Literature

Ernie Pyle (1900–1945) was a Pulitzer Prize–winning journalist with the common touch. Renowned for profiling the lives of ordinary Americans, Pyle became a war correspondent when World War II began. His columns gave readers the feeling of what it was like to be a soldier on the front lines of the conflict. He reported from London during the fifty-seven days of daily German bombing known as the "Blitz." The Blitz was Hitler's attempt to crush the spirit of the British people by targeting the civilian population directly. Schools, churches, and hospitals were all destroyed, and the city was in flames. Pyle describes the scene: "Flames seemed to whip hundreds of feet into the air. Pinkish-white smoke ballooned upward in a great cloud, and out of this cloud there gradually took shape

— so faintly at first that we weren't sure we saw correctly — the gigantic dome of St. Paul's Cathedral."

On May 10, 1941, three thousand civilians were incinerated by Luftwaffe bombs. Yet despite the constant, merciless pounding and the almost complete destruction of their city, Londoners were un-bowed. Indeed, they came together and strengthened their resolve to defeat the Nazi enemy. How were people able to rally under such appalling conditions?

Leadership! Specifically, the leadership of Winston Churchill. Churchill's electrifying speeches boosted the confidence and cour-age of the British people. He also practiced the art of connection in subtler ways. When he was named prime minister, his first act was to reach out to the former head of state, Neville Chamberlain, who had fallen from popularity due to his unsuccessful attempts at diplomacy with Germany. Churchill was extremely gracious in his treatment of his predecessor, inviting Chamberlain and his family to stay at 10 Downing Street, the British prime minister's residence, for as long as they liked. Churchill's kindness and consideration helped make Chamberlain an ally who ultimately helped support some of Churchill's most important legislation in Parliament.

How is it that one man could inspire a whole nation in the face of such adversity? Churchill was indeed a glowworm. He radiated confidence, character, and courage in the face of pervasive gloom. His positive message was contagious, and it spread through Britain to help save the nation and ultimately all of civilization as we know it.

Emotions Are Contagious

Every man is like the company he keeps.

— EURIPIDES (480–406 BCE), Greek playwright

Nicholas A. Christakis and James H. Fowler, authors of *Connected: The Surprising Power of Our Social Networks and How They Shape*

Our Lives, are on the forefront of "computational social science," a revolutionary new way to understand our relationships. This evolving discipline is based on the observation that our emotions are contagious. They're studying how the contagion spreads, for better or worse, affecting everything from our weight and alcohol consumption to our sleep patterns and general happiness.

Computational social science validates the classic observation of author and motivational speaker Jim Rohn (1930–2009): "You are the average of the five people you spend the most time with." In other words, if those five people are alcoholic, obese, or depressed, then you are more susceptible to those conditions, but if those five people are healthy, happy, and fit, then you are more likely to be so too.

Christakis is optimistic about leveraging our understanding of social connectedness to bring out the best in ourselves and others. He explains, "The amazing thing about social networks, unlike other networks that are almost as interesting — networks of neurons or genes or stars or computers — is that the nodes of a social network — the entities, the components — are themselves sentient, acting individuals who can respond to the network and actually form it themselves." And when Christakis says, "sentient, acting individuals who can respond to the network and actually form it themselves," he's talking about us!

Marco Iacoboni comments: "There is a lot of mirroring going on between people when they interact socially. This makes sense to psychologists who study emotional contagion, providing insight into the way feelings and behavior spread from one person to another." As sentient beings we can form and respond to our networks, both real and virtual, intelligently.

Which Emotions Do You Want to Catch and Spread?

All souls may be created equal, but some personalities are much more enriching to be around than others. "Big Mike" Schwegman is one of the instructors at the Dragonwell kung fu studio, where I train. Raised in a neighborhood where academic achievement wasn't emphasized, he graduated high school in 1988, and over the years he's driven cabs, remodeled kitchens, and sold sports memorabilia. Now he runs a successful carpet-cleaning business.

Mike has an impressive breadth and depth of knowledge about martial arts, philosophy, and life. Given his erudition on a range of subjects, I was surprised to learn that he hadn't attended college. Last night we were practicing "coiling silk" exercises, which are designed to generate more flexible strength and effortless power. Mike, who weighs in at around 230 pounds, moved lightly and gracefully in demonstrating the exercises, while offering a clear and accessible explanation of the complex internal dynamics of the movements.

I decided to ask him something that I'd been wondering about while appreciating his teaching over the last few months. Here's the conversation that ensued:

MJG: Hey, Mike, how did you get so smart?

MIKE: (*Laughing*) Well, it's a good question, 'cause when I was younger, I was a real f--k-up!

MJG: So how did you become the Renaissance man that you are today?

MIKE: Well, I don't know about that! But when I was in my early twenties, somebody, and I can't really even remember who it was, told me something that absolutely changed my life. He said, "Hang out with people who are better than you. Find people who are smarter than you, and hang out with them."

And for some reason I listened. I stopped hanging out with the crowd I used to go drinking with, and I actually tried to find smarter people. That's how I found my martial arts teacher, and that's what set me on the path to a much better life. And the great thing is that, as a father, I've been able to pass that idea on to my son.

And I'm not always smart. I do dumb stuff more than I'd like.

MJG: Smart people are aware of the dumb stuff they do. The people we need to worry about are those who are oblivious.

Big Mike discovered that his neighborhood cohorts weren't bringing out his best. He realized that he had to go out of his way to find more positive influences. Like Mike, Keith McFarland, who is now a successful author and consultant on leadership and business strategy, learned early in life that connecting with smart, creative, positive people is a critical key to success and fulfillment. Raised in a trailer in northern New Mexico across from a 7-Eleven store managed by his dad, Keith developed a method for uplifting his life that he playfully terms "constructive stalking."

· Keith explains: "I literally would stalk people. I'd identify great, positive, inspiring people such as entrepreneurs, authors, professors, and I'd follow them around. I'd save my pennies and then invite them to lunch."

After working his way through college, Keith got an MBA from Pepperdine University and at age twenty-six became associate dean of Pepperdine's Business School. He is the author of *The Breakthrough Company: How Everyday Companies Become Extraordinary Performers* and *Bounce: The Art of Turning Tough Times into Triumph*.

When asked to share an example of constructive stalking, Keith explained that one of the people he was determined to meet was the legendary journalist, editor, and author of *Anatomy of an Illness as Perceived by the Patient: Reflections on Healing and Regeneration*, Norman Cousins. Keith says, "I had to figure out an angle to meet him. I knew he had a new book coming out, so I volunteered to organize a book signing for him."

Keith arranged to go to Cousins's home for a planning meeting, but when he got there, Cousins was on the telephone. Cousins gave Keith a glass of water and asked him to wait. Keith waited for seventy-five minutes, feeling increasingly frustrated that Cousins was talking on the phone rather than being available for all of his questions.

At the end of seventy-five minutes, Cousins came out and apologized to Keith, explaining that he had to run to another meeting. Keith asked Cousins why he was on the phone the whole time, and he replied: "Well, when I survived my illness despite receiving a terminal diagnosis, I committed to be available for counseling for anyone who gets a terminal diagnosis. I just spent the last seventy-five minutes talking to patients who needed a ray of hope in the darkness of their despair."

Keith marvels, "What a humbling, but also inspiring experience that turned out to be. I learned more from Cousins's actions than I ever could have from anything he said."

Being around great people like Norman Cousins is, as Keith discovered, simultaneously humbling and inspiring. Greatness is contagious! The great American writer Mark Twain (1835–1910) observed, "Really great people make you feel that you too can become great." Poet Henry Wadsworth Longfellow (1807–82) wrote:

> Lives of great men all remind us
> We can make our lives sublime,
> And, departing, leave behind us
> Footprints on the sands of time.

When we study the lives of great men and women, we discover, among their most distinguishing characteristics, that they all intentionally sought positive role models. Churchill, for example, modeled himself after his heroes, including Admiral Horatio Nelson, T. E. Lawrence, and his father, Lord Randolph Churchill.

Most species learn by imitation. Baby ducks, for example, learn to walk by imitating their mothers. We develop significant aspects of our behavioral repertoire by imitating our parents and the other individuals with whom we spend the most time while growing up. One of the great benefits of being an adult is that we can consciously choose what and whom to imitate.

In addition to identifying the leaders you'd like to meet in the coming year and stalking them constructively, you can also spend time with great leaders virtually. Churchill, Mandela, Aung San Suu Kyi, and Mother Teresa, among many others, are all waiting for you on YouTube. The people with whom you spend the most time, in person and virtually, are like a hall of mirrors, reflecting and magnifying attitudes, qualities, and behaviors, for better or worse.

To Be a Glowworm, Avoid Tapeworms

Think about the five people with whom you spend the most time and consider whether you need to make some changes. As well as constructively stalking positive people, you will also want to prune the negative ones from your life.

In other words, to the extent possible, minimize or eliminate altogether interactions with negative influences. Although it's commendable to look for the best in others and to be compassionate toward all sentient beings, even those who may drain your energy, *it doesn't mean you need to continue your association with them.*

Is there anyone in your life, personally or professionally, who speaks to you in a demeaning fashion? Who violates your personal space? Do you sometimes witness or find yourself on the receiving end of insults, sarcasm, threats, or profanity? What happens to your energy and your productivity after an encounter with someone like this?

Robert Sutton is a professor of management science and engineering at Stanford and the author of *The No Asshole Rule: Building a Civilized Workplace and Surviving One That Isn't*. Sutton responds to the many inquiries he receives about why he chose to use a word in his title that might be offensive to many people: "I know the term offends some people, but nothing else captures the emotional wallop." Sutton explains why he wanted to deliver the wallop: "My father always told me to avoid assholes at all costs, no matter how rich or powerful they might be, because I would catch their nastiness and impose it on others. I learned, as an organizational psychologist, that his advice is supported by research on 'emotional contagion': if you work for a jerk, odds are you will become one." Sutton adds that those who practice incivility and demeaning behavior do terrible damage to others and to their companies.

Sutton's father's advice is validated by other contemporary research. Christine Porath, professor at the McDonough School of Business at Georgetown University, and her colleagues have conducted extensive studies into the effects of the kind of behavior that Sutton's father warned him to avoid. It really is contagious! One of her studies showed that "25 percent of managers who admitted to having behaved badly said they were uncivil because their leaders — their own role models — were rude. If employees see that those who have climbed the corporate ladder tolerate or embrace uncivil behavior, they're likely to follow suit."

Porath, author of *Mastering Civility: A Manifesto for the Workplace*, and her colleagues validate Sutton's conclusion that people who practice incivility and abusive behavior toward others aren't just offensive; they're destructive. After surveying more than fourteen thousand people from a wide range of organizations, they found that organizations that tolerate incivility suffer greater turnover and have trouble attracting and retaining the best people, are less creative and innovative, and lose customers and weaken their brand. (People are less likely to buy from a company with an employee they perceive as rude, even if the rudeness isn't directed at them.) Porath sums it up: "Incivility is expensive."

But maybe you're still wondering: Doesn't incivility and ruthless behavior help some people get ahead? Sutton responds, "Even though there are occasions when being an asshole helps people and companies 'win,' my view is that if you are a winner and an asshole, you are still an asshole and I don't want to be around you."

Like Big Mike and Keith, you can make positive choices about who you want in your life, and maybe, even more important, *who you don't want in your life*. Those choices help to form who you will become. By carefully considering who you want to spend your time with, you will evolve into being the kind of person with whom others want to spend their time.

And even if it isn't always possible to end your association with those who are far from ideal role models, you can nevertheless choose to respond consciously and proactively. As legendary Chinese philosopher Confucius (551–479 BCE) advises: "If I am walking with two other men, each of them will serve as my teacher. I will pick out the good points of one and imitate them, and the bad points of the other and correct them in myself."

Emotions are contagious. You decide what you want to catch and also what you want to spread. How do you spread inspiration, trust, and creativity?

CHRIS'S SUPER POWER

As a psychotherapist, Chris Ranck is immersed in the contemplation of human nature on a daily basis. We recently discussed the issue, and she shared the following story.

Chris and her husband live on the ground floor of a beautiful old prewar building in New York City, with a semiprivate back door into a small hallway that leads to a door right out to the street. They share that back-door exit with the superintendent of the building, who also lives on the ground floor. Recently, they were being awakened by loud noises made by someone coming in and out of their shared hallway in the middle of the night.

Chris exclaims, "The old doors are squeaky and heavy, and they have to be slammed in order to be fully shut and then locked. This makes a hellish racket!"

Chris told me that she and her husband were both out of the apartment during the times the super was available, so she decided to write a note on a pretty card, asking the super to resolve the matter. Of course, as anyone who has ever lived in a New York apartment knows, rapport with the super can make a huge difference in the quality of life. Chris explains that she was "holding her breath" as she penned the note, but that she believed he was a well-meaning person. Here's the note she put under his door:

> I'm writing because I doubt that I will see you today. Recently someone has been using the back door between 1:00 and 2:30 AM — for several nights. I can tell that they are trying to be quiet, but it is just impossible with those old doors, and it has been waking us up. We've had a few restless nights. I know you're a very thoughtful person, and we're not trying to be old poops, LOL! Could I respectfully suggest that the back door not be used by any of us after 11:00 PM (except, of course, in emergencies)? Could you let me know if that is workable for your household? I wanted to let you know what's happening on our side of the door.
>
> Thanks. We appreciate your consideration.

Chris was anxious when she didn't receive a response for several days, but she did notice that the nighttime interruptions stopped. A few days later she ran into the super in the lobby. He gave her a big hug, said that her note had "truly warmed his heart," and asked her to wait a moment so he could bring his girlfriend to say hello. The girlfriend, who had recently moved in, presented Chris with a beautiful bouquet of roses and explained that it was her eighteen-year-old son who had been using the back door in the middle of the night, and that they were trying to teach him to be considerate and think of others, so the note had not only been timely but actually helpful in providing a lesson for him.

When I asked Chris how she felt about this, she responded, "I was nearly speechless, a little overwhelmed, and teary-eyed, and we all hugged. But it did remind me of what I have always believed: that if you assume the best of people and act accordingly, they will not disappoint you."

Then she added, "And I have never heard another peep from the other side of the door since."

The Pygmalion Effect

A man should never be appointed to a managerial position
if his vision focuses on people's weaknesses
rather than on their strengths.
— PETER DRUCKER, *The Practice of Management* (1954)

In a classic *Seinfeld* moment, Elaine tells Jerry, "I will never understand people." Jerry responds, "They're the worst."

Are people the worst, or the best? Are we fundamentally good or bad? Angels incarnate or vicious animals? Our view of human nature has profound implications for the form of government we choose, the way we run a business, and the way we conduct our lives. Whatever theory you hold, the important practical question for leaders, parents, and partners is: How do I bring out the best in others?

Numerous studies in academic, military, and corporate situations reveal that the expectations of a teacher, drill sergeant, or boss affect performance significantly: positive expectations yield better performance; with negative expectations, performance declines.

For example, a cadre of army drill sergeants were told that their next class of recruits was below average in ability. At the end of basic training, that group of recruits performed 25 percent below average. The drill sergeants were then told that their next crop of recruits was above average in ability. At the end of basic training, that group performed 25 percent above average. When the sergeants were debriefed after the experiment and told that both groups were average in their ability, they refused to believe it. Their expectations became their reality.

In Greek mythology, Pygmalion was a sculptor who became enamored of one of his own carvings, which then came to life. British author George Bernard Shaw (1856–1950) penned a play that was a takeoff on this theme in which a phoneticist, Professor Higgins, bets Colonel Pickering, a linguist, that he can pass off a flower girl as a duchess by training her to speak properly (adapted as the modern classic *My Fair Lady*). After her months of training and then success at an aristocratic party, Eliza Doolittle, Shaw's heroine, explains to Colonel Pickering how expectation has influenced her: "You see, really and truly, apart from the things anyone can pick up (the dressing and the proper way of speaking, and so on), the difference between a lady and a flower girl is not how she behaves, but how she's treated. I shall always be a flower girl to Professor Higgins, because he always treats me as a flower girl and always will; but I know I can be a lady to you because you always treat me as a lady and always will."

The notion that positive expectations tend to elevate performance is known as the *Pygmalion effect*. It is also called the *Rosenthal effect*, after Robert Rosenthal, the pioneer of research into interpersonal self-fulfilling prophecies. After almost fifty years of study in both the laboratory and the field, Rosenthal observes: "We have learned that when teachers have been led to expect better intellectual performance from their students, they tend to get it. When coaches are led to expect better athletic performance from their athletes, they tend to get it."

In one of his original studies at an elementary school in the San Francisco area, Rosenthal chose a few children randomly and told their teachers that these children would demonstrate dramatic improvements in IQ. After two years the children's IQ conformed to the teachers' expectations.

Was the improvement a function of some mystical transference? No. The effect is mediated through nonverbal cues. Rosenthal explains, "It's not magic, it's not mental telepathy." He found that "expectations affect teachers' moment-to-moment interactions with the children they teach in a thousand almost invisible ways. Teachers give the students that they expect to succeed more time to answer questions, more specific feedback, and more approval: they consistently touch, nod, and smile at those kids more."

In other words, there's valid research behind the idea that if you look for the best in others, you will usually find it. The opposite is also true. Negative expectation seems to yield negative results. If you believe that people can't be trusted, you will probably find yourself surrounded by untrustworthy people. And people may not trust you either, since your philosophy of human nature obviously must apply to yourself as well.

THE PYGMALION EFFECT FOR LEADERS

After correlating scientific research with his own extensive case studies, former Harvard Business School professor J. Sterling Livingston (1916–2010) reports:

- What managers expect of subordinates and the way they treat them largely determine their performance and career progress.
- A unique characteristic of superior managers is the ability to create high performance expectations that subordinates fulfill.
- Subordinates, more often than not, appear to do what they believe they are expected to do.

The work of Rosenthal, Livingston, and many others makes it clear that when a manager, boss, or supervisor believes that her people are high performers, then those people are much more likely to perform at a higher level. If she is convinced that her people are subpar, then they will probably underperform.

Expectations become self-fulfilling prophecies for better or for worse. They're important in interacting with superintendents and critical for being an effective supervisor. If you don't expect much from yourself, then you may find yourself surrounded by people who don't inspire you to be your best.

On the other hand, if you practice constructive stalking and choose your milieu consciously, surrounding yourself with people who bring out the best in you, you are much more likely to manifest the best. As you do, others then want to be around you, because you've learned the secret of being a glowworm!

The Greatest Point of Leverage

CONTEMPLATE AND, IF NECESSARY, ADJUST THE EXPECTATION YOU HAVE FOR YOURSELF.

Treat a man as he is, and he will remain as he is.
Treat a man as he ought to be, and you help him become
what he is capable of becoming.
— JOHANN WOLFGANG VON GOETHE (1749–1832),
German writer, scientist, and statesman

Your emotions, and your expectations, are contagious. Contemplate the way your expectations for others may be affecting them for better or for worse. Consider how you might adjust those expectations to generate more connection and inspiration.

And the most important point of leverage for this essential

element of leadership is *to contemplate and, if necessary, adjust the expectation you have for yourself.* This is the greatest point of leverage, because to make changes in your milieu, to "eliminate the deadbeats," to constructively stalk positive role models, to devote your time and energy to studying the lives and lessons of great leaders, and to generate more connection and inspiration in others, you've got to believe, or at least act as though you believe, in yourself.

You can change your life by changing the way you think about yourself and your potential. There are two unproductive, but common, extremes when it comes to self-expectation. One is to expect perfect results from yourself (and others) at all times. This causes constant unhappiness and frustration. The other is to not expect enough from yourself (or others), because you feel unworthy.

In the first chapter we learned the importance of embracing humility. True humility emerges from a sense of wonder and awe. It's an appreciation that our time on earth is limited but that there's something timeless at the core of every being. Embracing humility liberates us from the egotism that drives both perfectionism and self-sabotage, opening us to a deeper experience of self-worth.

When it comes to changing the way you think about yourself so that you can bring out your best and then the best in others, remember that connection with your own soul is the only reliable source of self-worth. Real self-esteem isn't a condition of the ego; it's a connection with something greater.

It's easy to forget this when you are struggling with adverse circumstances, but in a way that is often surprising, your soul may be more available for you to experience when you are suffering. Eckhart Tolle, author of *The Power of Now*, and Byron Katie, author of *Loving What Is: 4 Questions That Can Change Your Life*, are two contemporary spiritual teachers who experienced awakenings out of the depths of depression. What they and many other seekers from all traditions have discovered is that whole-hearted surrender of the separate self, the ego, is life-changing. This surrender is also the core of the transformational power of twelve-step programs.

Byron Katie counsels, "Do you want to meet the love of your life? Look in the mirror." Katie isn't referring to the body you see in the mirror, but rather to the awareness that is seeing. Poet Kahlil Gibran (1883–1931) reflects: "Beauty is eternity gazing at itself in a mirror. But you are eternity and you are the mirror." If you look in the mirror with appreciation for the radiant awareness that is the essence of your being, then that's what other people's mirror neurons will be reflecting when they see you.

This is the spiritual element of the art of connection.

The author of *Autobiography of a Yogi*, Paramahansa Yogananda (1893–1952), defined spiritual consciousness as the "realization of God's presence in oneself and in every other living being." Most of us frequently forget this. It's especially easy to forget that others are reflections of the Divine when they act in ways that seem obnoxious. So create as many reminders as possible.

In India and in most yoga classes in the West, people raise their hands, palms up, at the level of the heart, make a small bow, and smile as they greet each other with the word *Namaste*, "I bow to the spirit in you." Start and finish every day with a *Namaste* to yourself.

3

Achieve the
Three Liberations

The contemplation of things as they are, without error or confusion, without substitution or imposture, is in itself a nobler thing than a whole harvest of inventions.

— FRANCIS BACON (1561–1626), British philosopher

I n 1973, I enrolled in a ten-month residential course at the International Academy for Continuous Education in England. J. G. Bennett (1897–1974), the founder and main teacher, had devoted his life to exploring the wisdom traditions of the world and did his best to pass on what he had learned.

The First Liberation: Freedom from Like and Dislike

In one of his talks, Bennett urged us to liberate ourselves from "like and dislike." He emphasized, "Overcoming like and dislike is the first practical step out of the dream world." He asked us to consider:

What is there in our nature that is slave to like and dislike?
How easy is it to break free from that slavery?
What is opened up for us then?

I've contemplated these questions for more than forty years. It isn't easy to break free from this slavery, because it is hardwired into our brains. Our brain stem and limbic system conspire to guarantee that we will automatically view most phenomena with regard to their potential for benefit or harm, as friend or foe, good or bad, right or wrong. This binary filter is the default setting of the human brain, and its original purpose was to aid us in survival. (One can only wonder, though, about the evolutionary benefits of our modern penchant for needing to respond to everything we see on websites with a "like" or "dislike," a "thumbs-up" or a "thumbs-down"!)

Many people confuse the notion of doing what they like and avoiding what they don't like with freedom. Bennett emphasized that real freedom is predicated on cultivating awareness of our habitual likes and dislikes and then choosing our responses based on our conscious intention.

Bennett introduced us to a practice for cultivating that freedom known today as *mindfulness*, usually defined as intentional, non-judgmental awareness of the present moment. He guided us to view ourselves objectively and to practice "nonjudgmental awareness" (NJA).

Over the years when I'd notice my tendency to judge almost everything and everyone instantaneously, I'd chide myself by reflecting, "I suck at NJA." But gradually it became apparent that I could accept my tendency to judge everything without judging myself for having that tendency. In other words, overcoming like and dislike isn't about eradicating or suppressing judgments; rather, it's a function of becoming aware of those judgments as they arise and subjecting them to thoughtful reflection.

A turning point for my realization of this powerful truth came one day just after lunch at Bennett's academy. While on cleanup duty in the dining room, I came across a particularly messy area where someone had left significant detritus from his or her meal on the table. After I began to mentally excoriate the slob, I realized that I was cleaning my own place! Although I felt shame initially, eventually I was able to laugh at foibles like this and began to feel more compassion for myself and others.

As I freed myself gradually from the counterproductive tendency to judge myself for judging everything, a new world of inner freedom and peace emerged, and a door opened to a more creative way to build relationships. Learning to *suspend* judgment of self and others, to separate my observation of what's happening in an interaction from my *evaluation* of the interaction, liberated tremendous energy for understanding and connecting.

If you want to liberate your creative intelligence to enrich all your relationships, then practice what Francis Bacon calls the "contemplation of things as they are, without substitution or imposture, without error or confusion." In other words, cultivate the ability to differentiate observations from evaluations. An observation is a statement of fact based on sensory evidence, that is, something that you see, hear, or touch. An evaluation is an interpretation or judgment of those facts. Another way to think of evaluation is that it is an opinion.

Observation or Evaluation?

J. Krishnamurti once remarked that observing without
evaluating is the highest form of human intelligence.
When I first read this statement, the thought
"What nonsense!" shot through my mind before
I realized that I had just made an evaluation.
— MARSHALL ROSENBERG (1934–2015), American psychologist
and founder of the Center for Nonviolent Communication

When we confuse evaluation and observation, we interfere with our ability to consider our present circumstances in a conscious and creative way. Moreover, evaluative language often generates a defensive response from the person at whom it is directed.

Let's explore the difference with an exercise adapted from the work of Marshall Rosenberg. Please contemplate the following statements and consider whether they are observations or evaluations:

1. Roger is the most judgmental person I've ever met.
2. My boss is awesome.
3. Compared to the other cars, the green Prius appears to be going slowly in the fast lane.
4. Nancy closed her eyes and started snoring while we were watching the safety video.
5. The security guard at the job site is a jerk.
6. My direct report is a slob.
7. Jack is a workaholic.
8. Alice told me that I look ridiculous in my new uniform.
9. Jim never listens to me.
10. My partner isn't good at distinguishing evaluations from observations.

Here are my thoughts on whether these statements are observations or evaluations. Do you agree or disagree?

1. Roger is the most judgmental person I've ever met.
   Evaluation. Modifiers such as *most, least, best,* and *worst* usually indicate that an evaluation is being made. An observation might be: "The last three times I spoke with Roger, he told me what he didn't like about his coworkers, friends, and wife."
2. My boss is awesome.
   Evaluation. Terms like *awesome, dreadful, fabulous,* and *wonderful* are all judgmental words. An observation might be: "My boss listened to my suggestion in last week's meeting

and implemented it today. Then he complimented me and gave me a raise."

3. Compared to the other cars, the green Prius appears to be going slowly in the fast lane.

   Observation.

4. Nancy closed her eyes and started snoring while we were watching the safety video.

   Observation.

5. The security guard at the job site is a jerk.

   Evaluation. *Jerk* is a pejorative term; it represents a judgment. An observation might be: "The security guard raised his voice and shook his fist at me."

6. My direct report is a slob.

   Evaluation. *Slob*, also pejorative, represents a judgment. An observation might be: "My direct report had burrito stains on his shirt and his shoes were untied."

7. Jack is a workaholic.

   Evaluation. *Workaholic* implies a judgment. An observation might be: "Jack has spent more than seventy hours at the office each week this month and hasn't taken a vacation in two years."

8. Alice told me that I look ridiculous in my new uniform.

   Observation. Alice made the evaluation.

9. Jim never listens to me.

   Evaluation. Words such as *never* and *always* usually indicate that an evaluation has taken place. An observation might be: "The last four times I met with Jim, he was texting when we spoke."

10. My partner isn't good at distinguishing evaluations from observations.

    Evaluation. *Isn't good at* is judgmental. An observation

might be: "My partner and I disagree on the distinction between evaluations and observations."

As we free ourselves from reflexive, unconscious evaluations
and cultivate the ability to observe accurately and objectively, we
strengthen our discernment. Many folks think the way to do this
is to refrain from having likes and dislikes, to be "neutral" about
everything. They forget that it is not possible for human beings
to "turn off" the hardwiring. What they are doing in the name of
mindfulness is suppressing their likes and dislikes and pretending
that everything is the same, convinced that they are beyond making
assessments of right and wrong.

Suppression doesn't work. It takes patience, humility, curiosity,
and commitment to become aware of our automatic evaluative con-
ditioning. The secret is to learn to monitor and acknowledge these
tendencies without acting them out or getting trapped in negative
self-judgment based on our habit of judging others.

In the movie *Analyze This*, Billy Crystal plays Dr. Sobel, a
psychiatrist who is attempting to get the notorious mobster Paul Vitti
(played by Robert De Niro) to express his feelings in a nonjudgmental way to a rival crime boss, Primo Sindone (Chazz Palminteri). De
Niro is hilarious when he awkwardly attempts to empathize with his
rival's unmet needs, and it isn't long before he explodes in a tirade of
graphic threats. Learning to express oneself without evaluation and
with empathy is usually awkward and difficult at first. Like many
other skills, it takes practice and patience.

Marshall Rosenberg explains that when he first began to practice
speaking without making evaluations or demands, but still attempting to accurately express his feelings and underlying needs, he was
often met with impatience by people close to him. In one instance
his son complained that he was too slow and awkward in his communication, so Marshall responded, "Let me tell you what I can say
quickly: 'Do it my way or I'll kick your butt!'"

Marshall's son responded, "Take your time, Dad. Take your time."

Nonjudgmental awareness doesn't imply that you can't have an opinion about whom you like, which wine you prefer, or which candidate you think is better qualified for office. Rather, it liberates awareness so that your opinions are less likely to be projections of your prejudices. As we free ourselves from automatic, unconscious, binary responses, we invite a deeper possibility of awareness.

Of course, sometimes judging others can just be fun. The question is: Are you aware of what you are doing and why?

In a playfully wicked fashion, poet and all-around critic Dorothy Parker (1893–1967) proffered the invitation: "If you can't say something good about someone, sit right here by me." Oscar Wilde made judging others into an art form. In *Lady Windermere's Fan* (1893), Lord Darlington quips, "It is absurd to divide people into good and bad. People are either charming or tedious." But even Parker and Wilde might concur that inner freedom and compassion are the wellsprings of real charm.

The Second Liberation: Freedom from Taking Things Personally

Patience serves us against insults precisely as clothes do
against the cold. For if you multiply your garments
as the cold increases, that cold cannot hurt you;
in the same way increase your patience under great offences,
and they cannot hurt your feelings.
— LEONARDO DA VINCI

It takes time to cultivate patience and the ability to see things as they are. First, we liberate ourselves from the tendency to view the world exclusively from a limiting binary filter, cultivating a consciousness that is more objective. This objectivity also allows us to avoid taking things personally when it isn't constructive to do so. We can be

open and accessible without being attached to what the poet Rumi
(1207–73) calls the "wind of personal reaction." He writes:

> When a wind of personal reaction comes,
> I do not go along with it.
> There are many winds full of anger,
> and lust and greed. They move the rubbish around,
> but the solid mountain of our true nature stays where it's
> always been.

The solid mountain of your true nature is the place from which you
can make fair, objective assessments and unprejudiced decisions that
build trust and inspire loyalty.

Along with Big Mike, Quannah Lee is one of the instructors at
our kung fu studio. His father is the founder of the school, so Quannah, a.k.a. "Q," has grown up in the discipline and is an excellent
teacher and practitioner at only twenty-four years of age. He also
builds beautiful handmade electric guitars, plays in a progressive
metal band, and works five nights a week as a waiter in a high-end
restaurant. He happened to mention that he had a big night of tips
recently, and I asked him his secret. It turns out that one of the other
students in the class is also working as a waiter, and we all discussed
the keys to success. The consensus? Connecting with guests by empathizing with their needs and not taking anything personally are
essentials for survival and success.

Q has been waiting tables since he was sixteen. Shy and introverted, he was afraid to talk to people when he started, but realized
that he had to learn to be more gregarious. He tried hard to sound
friendly and welcoming to his customers, but after a while he relaxed
when he realized that being a successful waiter just meant that he
needed to put his own concerns aside and focus on trying to help his
guests "get what they want, get what they need."

Q recently served a big group. The policy in his restaurant, a standard policy in most restaurants, is to add a set service charge for groups larger than six. Q told us that this particular group appeared to be a large family and that the patriarch was upset by this policy. Q attempted to gently explain to them that it was standard. But somehow one of the sons took exception and began to yell at him. Q recounts, "He actually shouted at me, 'Don't you dare talk to my father that way! I will kick your ass!'"

I asked Q how he dealt with the threat. With delightful nonchalance he explained: "I thought this guy must be having a really rough day. I just don't take anything personally. You can't last in this business if you do. I just shrugged it off and didn't react. I went about my business and took everyone's order. They had a nice evening."

Since Q has a devastating, lightning-fast reverse-spin kick that makes a loud thud on our big heavy bag when he sends it catapulting toward the wall, it's really lucky for that guest that he doesn't take threats personally. The ability to not take things personally is usually associated with maturity, and it's unusual in someone as young as Quannah, but then again his father's school emphasizes a Zen-like inner freedom in the face of conflict.

"When you're twenty," according to proverbial wisdom, "you care what everyone thinks, when you're forty you stop caring what everyone thinks, and when you're sixty you realize no one was ever thinking about you in the first place." Musing on the role of maturity in not taking things personally, author Pearl S. Buck (1892–1973) writes, "Well, perhaps one has to be very old before one learns how to be amused rather than shocked."

It's amusing to consider that the reasons for not taking things personally aren't just that it's wise and mature and that it almost always results in better outcomes and more harmonious relationships; in most cases when people seem to be insulting or obnoxious, their behavior is more about them — a function of their own mood — than it is about you.

Most people, especially those who act out antisocial behaviors, are lost in their own patterns of association. Chances are that Quannah's rude guest was trying to win his father's approval or showing off for his girlfriend; maybe his boss yelled at him earlier in the day or perhaps he has a brain tumor. It's hard to know specifically why people do what they do, but in general it's a good policy to keep in mind Goethe's observation: "Misunderstandings and neglect create more confusion in this world than trickery and malice. At any rate, the last two are certainly much less frequent." In contemporary language this notion is expressed in the maxim: "Never attribute to malice or aggression that which is adequately explained by conceit or stupidity."

As Don Miguel Ruiz explains in *The Four Agreements: A Practical Guide to Personal Wisdom*: "Nothing other people do is because of you. It is because of themselves. All people live in their own dream, in their own mind."

Now, I confess that my first reaction is to take everything personally. When I feel affronted, insulted, or attacked, my battle stations are mobilized immediately. In those first crucial moments of reaction, I've learned to bring my attention to my breathing and to slow it down. I adjust my posture so it's free from the fight-or-flight orientation, and then I contemplate this transformative question: "How would I think/feel about this action/comment if I did not take it personally?"

As you cultivate the ability to be free from taking things personally, it's important to remember that almost everyone you meet *will* take everything personally. That's why it's so important to be able to speak to others without using evaluative language. That's part of how you will distinguish yourself as a leader in this world.

The Third Liberation: Freedom from Blaming and Complaining

Leadership consists of nothing but taking responsibility
for everything that goes wrong and giving
your subordinates credit for everything that goes well.
— DWIGHT D. EISENHOWER (1890–1969),
thirty-fourth president of the United States

Realizing that all souls are created equal and that misunderstanding
is pandemic, we embrace humility. Humility inspires curiosity, so
instead of assuming we understand, we seek to understand. Seeking to understand, we learn to separate observation from evaluation. Learning to contemplate things as they are without error or
confusion while not taking things personally sets the stage for the
next liberation — freedom from blame, self-pity, and complaining,
so you can take full responsibility for your effectiveness in the art of
connection.

I was introduced to this idea as a teenager when I read *Man's
Search for Meaning* by Viktor Frankl. It changed my life. Frankl
(1905–97) was an Austrian psychiatrist imprisoned in a concentration camp by the Nazis during World War II, where he and his fellow inmates lived under the most degrading conditions imaginable.
Miraculously, Frankl discovered that although his captors had taken
his external liberty, they could not deprive him of his inner freedom,
his freedom to use his imagination as he wished.

Frankl focused on finding meaning through loving-kindness toward others despite his hellish surroundings. He survived, helped
inspire many others to survive, and then became an inspiration to
a generation. His story gave me hope. If he could find meaning
through a sense of personal responsibility in the worst possible conditions, then maybe I, in my far more comfortable circumstances,
could do so as well.

The notion of personal responsibility is at the heart of the heroic spirit. It is the inspiration underlying the achievements of great leaders throughout history from Nelson Mandela to Mother Teresa, from Winston Churchill to Aung San Suu Kyi.

In a speech at Harvard University in 1943, as World War II threatened Britain's survival, Churchill said, "The price of greatness is responsibility." In her Nobel Peace Prize acceptance speech, Aung San Suu Kyi said, "Every thought, every word, and every action that adds to the positive and the wholesome is a contribution to peace. Each and every one of us is capable of making such a contribution."

Personal responsibility is also at the heart of many of the world's great spiritual teachings. As the sage J. Krishnamurti (1895–1986) expressed it: "The central fact [is] that we, as individuals...are totally responsible for the whole state of the world. We are each one of us responsible for every war because of the aggressiveness of our own lives, because of our nationalism, our selfishness, our gods, our prejudices, our ideals, all of which divide us." Krishnamurti explains the challenge we face in taking responsibility:

> There is no guide, no teacher, no authority. There is only you — your relationship with others and with the world — there is nothing else. When you realize this, it either brings great despair, from which comes cynicism and bitterness, or, in facing the fact that you and nobody else is responsible for the world and for yourself, for what you think, what you feel, how you act, all self-pity goes. Normally we thrive on blaming others, which is a form of self-pity.

When you're in a concentration camp like Frankl, defending Western civilization by surviving nightly bombings like Churchill, imprisoned for thirty years like Mandela or for fifteen like Kyi, there's a powerful incentive to go within and find the strength to overcome despair and self-pity and to mobilize all your resources toward self-empowerment and inner liberation.

The challenge for most of us is that, because we live in

relatively comfortable circumstances, it is easy to forget this self-empowerment. As humorist P. J. O'Rourke observes: "One of the annoying things about believing in free will and individual responsibility is the difficulty of finding somebody to blame your problems on. And when you do find somebody, it's remarkable how often his picture turns up on your driver's license."

Unfortunately, our judicial system doesn't always help promote the value of personal responsibility. Here's a brief sample of some recent legal cases that made the news:

> A grown man in New York sued his parents for their "indifference" to his problems.
>
> A New Jersey school kicked a student off the track team for excessive absences, and his dad sued the county for $40 million.
>
> A grad student who received free tuition sued her Pennsylvania school over a grade.
>
> A Tennessee man sued Apple for his porn addiction.
>
> Two New Jersey men sued Subway because their "footlong" sandwiches fell short.

When things go wrong in our relationships at work or at home, it's too easy to engage in blame, self-pity, and complaining about others.

Watch a few episodes of *Real Housewives* (any city will do) or *Keeping Up with the Kardashians* on television, and you'll discover a streaming cornucopia of whining, self-pity, and blame, as the participants jockey to promote their product empires, memoirs, and self-help books. (At last count there were fourteen books published by "Real Housewives," including *Life Is Not a Reality Show*, by Kyle Richards, and *I Suck at Relationships So You Don't Have To*, by Bethenny Frankel.)

What makes these shows so popular? Psychologist Melanie Greenberg, writing for *Psychology Today*, confesses, "I've always felt secretly guilty about watching.... Would the superficial shenanigans of these privileged, Botoxed divas kill brain neurons or lead me to be ostracized by my PhD peers?"

The *Housewives*, *Kardashians*, and other so-called reality shows appeal for many reasons besides the opportunity they provide for us to, in Greenberg's words, "practice our skills at diagnosing mental-health problems." Greenberg explains that the appeal "is like reading the tabloids — the really juicy, sordid magazines we're too embarrassed to buy at the supermarket checkout stand."

Emotions are contagious. Voyeurism and envy are hypnotic. We all have an inner Kardashian and an inner Viktor Frankl. Sometimes we blame, whine, and complain, and other times we take responsibility and respond creatively to challenging situations. A transformational key to the art of connection is to become more aware of where you are on the continuum of personal responsibility and endeavor to respond as though all your communication and relationship challenges are opportunities for learning.

As poet and novelist Jorge Luis Borges (1899–1986) expressed it: "A writer — and, I believe, generally all persons — must think that whatever happens to him or her is a resource. All things have been given to us for a purpose, and an artist must feel this more intensely. All that happens to us, including our humiliations, our misfortunes, our embarrassments, all is given to us as raw material, as clay, so that we may shape our art."

We shape the art of connection by taking full responsibility for:

- accurately understanding others
- getting our message across to others
- whatever is achieved as a result

Blaming and complaining are usually symptoms of low self-esteem. As Rollo May noted in *Psychology and the Human Dilemma*: "When people feel their insignificance as individual persons, they also suffer an undermining of their sense of human responsibility."

Assess and nurture your responsibility by monitoring your attitudes as they are reflected in your language and notice where you are on the continuum. Classic lines that show when one's sense of responsibility has been undermined include:

"He *makes* me furious."
"If I've told you once, I've told you a thousand times."
"My wife/husband doesn't understand me."
"I can't get anyone at work to listen."
"There's nothing we can do about it."
"*They* won't let me."

WOULD YOU LIKE SOME CHEESE WITH THAT WHINE?

"My job stinks, my girlfriend's cheating on me, I've got a nasty case of athlete's foot that itches like you wouldn't believe, but hey, you know me, I can't complain."

This paraphrase of a hilarious routine by comedian Dom Irrera highlights the prevalence of — and the lack of awareness about — griping, grumbling, and groaning in everyday interactions. One recent report suggested that the average person complains once every minute while conversing. Although maybe they're complaining because, as another study showed, on average people are interrupted after eighteen seconds of speaking.

Indulging in or colluding with whining, complaining, and commiserating may damage your hippocampus (the place in your brain where images of hippopotamuses attending college are stored). There's also some indication that it raises baseline levels of stress and weakens your immune system. Like smoking, it's habit-forming, and it is detrimental to those who are around when you're doing it.

When you catch yourself indulging in any form of whining, blaming, complaining, or commiserating ("being miserable together"), do not attempt to change directly. Instead of grafting superficial "positive self-talk" on top of your current feelings, just observe or "witness" the behavior, without judging yourself. The difference is that now you are conscious of what you are doing, so you are free to *choose* to whine! Of course, once you are awake, whining starts to get a little boring, so have some fun exaggerating the whining, blaming, complaining, or commiserating.

Once you have acknowledged, accepted, and chuckled about the part of you that loves to whine, you are able to choose a more constructive orientation. Some reflections from the more creative end of the continuum include:

"Others may provide a stimulus for my feelings, but I'm in
     charge of my response."
"How can I alter my approach to generate better results?"
"I teach people how to treat me."
"I can't change others, but I can change the way I see them."
"How does what I detest about this person mirror something in my own character?"

These reflections are echoed in many writings about conscious leadership and enhanced awareness, but often in a somewhat pious and impractical way. In the real world, embracing the creative end of the continuum is challenging! Consider the notion: "Others may provide a stimulus for my feelings, but I'm in charge of my response." This is an empowering thought, but putting it into practice is challenging. I strive for equanimity and the ability to separate observation from evaluation and to avoid taking various slings and arrows personally. Still, when someone makes a promise and breaks it, which happens frequently as people become more distracted, I have to work really hard at not going ballistic with blame.

Recently a client in the software business for whom I had

conducted a successful seminar asked me to hold a series of dates for follow-up programs. We met in her office to discuss the programs and came to an agreement. We looked one another in the eye and shook hands, and she asked me to send a letter of agreement to confirm the dates and terms. I returned to my office and had the letter drafted and sent immediately. After a few days went by without a response, I resent the letter with a polite note. No response. I left a polite voice mail asking if there was any question or problem I could resolve to facilitate the confirmation. No response. I sent another nice note asking if the timing of the payment needed to be adjusted to make it easier for the client. No response.

It was very tempting to blame this person for what could easily be evaluated as an appalling lack of integrity. But what good would that have done? I could have said, "This *makes me* so angry," and then all the power over my inner state would have been ceded to this person. Look, I'm still not happy about this, but whenever I think about it, I choose to adjust my posture to full upright, breathe more deeply, smile, and let it go. In other words, I choose to free myself from the "wind of personal reaction" and affirm my connection with "the solid mountain of my true nature."

A few years ago I experienced another client disappearing act that would also be easy to label as *infuriating*. I had led a series of seminars for the CEO of a growing engineering firm. The feedback was positive, so I proposed that we work together on a longer-term basis. He said, "Yes!" and then disappeared. No response to repeated emails or voice mails. Nothing! Nada! I found myself ranting about what an objectionable character this guy was, but then I woke up and realized that all I was doing was marinating in my own stress hormones.

So I shifted out of blame and anger and thought in a more compassionate way about why I hadn't heard from him. I remembered that he had a daughter who was an international soccer player, and

I did an internet search. It turns out that she had broken her leg in a match in Europe, which her team lost in a heartbreaking way. I guessed that her dad was caught up in attending to her well-being. I wrote to him again, sent a few messages for his daughter about recovering from adversity, and offered to do a complimentary coaching session for her. I heard back from the CEO right away, and a few weeks later we signed a multiyear deal. I confess, I was really close to telling him off. I'm so glad I didn't! And I've still never heard anything from the software client.

In both of these cases it was easy to make an excoriating evaluation of the character of the person with whom I was interacting. For me, doing this creates a feeling of self-righteousness that seems as though it might help protect the part of me that feels hurt when I perceive that I'm being ignored. The problem is that it just doesn't work very well. Instead of focusing on how right I was and on how wrong the others were, I've learned to be curious about my VABEs (values, assumptions, beliefs, expectations) and the needs and values of others.

Upon reflection I realized that integrity, doing what one promises to do, is something that I value highly. I also have a need to feel that my contributions are recognized and appreciated. In both circumstances I was enthusiastic about the work we had done, looking forward to contributing further, and disappointed and bewildered when I received no response.

Recognizing this and honoring my own values allowed me the freedom to become curious about what might have led these two people not to respond. In the case of the engineering CEO, I realized that he was trying to meet his own deep need to take care of his daughter. By attuning to his deeper motivation, I was able to deepen our connection and generate a fulfilling, positive outcome.

In the case of the software CEO, I reflected that perhaps she may have been confronted with some new developments and was feeling overwhelmed. Had she made the agreement because she was uncomfortable saying no and in that moment her need to feel more comfortable was utmost? Since I still haven't heard from her, I don't know what her motivations were, but by contemplating in this more curious and compassionate way, it's easier to maintain my connection to her humanity. This allows me to have a sense of peace and power rather than anger and impotence, thereby allowing a deeper sense of connection with my true nature. And that connection leads to more resourcefulness and creativity.

Responsibility is a function of inner freedom, and inner freedom requires liberation from blame. We liberate ourselves from blame and make it possible to find creative ways to connect when we remember that, *although it may not always be apparent*, other people are doing their best to meet their human needs and express their VABEs (values, assumptions, beliefs, expectations) in any given moment.

In hell everyone blames everyone else for everything. In purgatory people take responsibility for the effectiveness of their communication about half the time. In heaven everyone embraces 100 percent responsibility.

The Greatest Point of Leverage

LEARN MARSHALL ARTS.

"Marshall Arts" is my playful name for nonviolent communication (NVC), a system of language and communication skills that reinforces the three liberations and allows us to stay connected with our own true nature and the true nature of others, even in difficult circumstances.

Growing up in a rough Detroit neighborhood, Marshall Rosenberg was surrounded by violence and thought that there must be a better way to resolve differences. This led him to train as a psychotherapist. Drawing on the wisdom of Carl Rogers and other

progressive psychologists and influenced by Gandhi's transformational application of nonviolence to facilitate social change, Rosenberg created the discipline of nonviolent communication (NVC).
Rosenberg figured out how all of us can incorporate the creative dynamics of a therapeutic dialogue into our everyday language.

NVC is predicated on the idea that humans share the same fundamental needs, but that we may differ in our strategies for expressing and fulfilling them. Rosenberg emphasizes, "Everything we do
is in service of our needs." NVC is the art of articulating our needs
in a way that inspires compassion in and connection with others,
while attuning to the needs of others, so that we may experience
more compassion for and connection with them.

Ironically, many people are put off by the idea of learning NVC,
because they react defensively to the name, protesting, "My communication is not violent!" or, "I am not violent. This doesn't apply
to me!" This concern has led some practitioners to rebrand NVC as
compassionate communication. We could also call it NCC, *new-context
communication,* as it reflects a manner of speaking that is more suited
to increasingly diverse and less hierarchical organizational contexts.

Understanding the original name of NVC becomes easier when
we know the deeper meaning of Gandhi's teaching of *ahimsa,* the
Sanskrit word usually translated as "nonviolence." The notion of
ahimsa is predicated on a fundamental spiritual truth: all creation is
one; everything, and everyone, is connected. Gandhi's practice of
nonviolence was based on his perception that all life is connected
and interdependent. Thus, violence against others is unthinkable for
those who consider others' welfare as important as their own.

Rosenberg applied NVC to mediate peaceful, creative resolutions between warring gangs, striking unions and their management,
and groups of Palestinians and Israelis. You can use it to enhance the
sense of joy and connection in your everyday relationships and to be
a more effective leader.

You can experience the benefits without sharing Gandhi's direct perception of the fundamental unity of creation. As you learn to reframe your language to liberate it from expressions of reflexive evaluation and blame, you may find yourself feeling more compassion and connection with life. Imagine how much energy might become available for creativity if it wasn't being channeled into blame!

The approach is based on four steps:

1. Identify what's actually happening in a given situation before evaluating it (separate observation from evaluation).
2. Recognize and be responsible for the feelings you experience in relationship to what you observe. Feelings may be *stimulated* by the words or actions of others, but are *caused* by the way you interpret what others do through the lens of your VABEs.
3. Attune to the deeper values and needs that underlie your feelings. Examples of deeper values and needs might include things like integrity, kindness, honesty, efficiency, frugality, generosity, understanding, recognition, creativity, peace, and connection.
4. Make clear requests rather than demands to greatly increase the likelihood that your needs will be met. (It isn't always easy to discern the difference between a request and a demand. The key is what happens when someone says no. If the no is met with a threat or punishment, then it wasn't a request.)

In addition to doing this simple four-step process for yourself, you endeavor to understand how others view a given situation, what their feelings are, what the needs underlying those feelings are, and what they might want to meet their needs. NVC invites us to contemplate this delightful question: "What if there were a way to change how I use and interpret language that might allow me to feel more connected to myself and others?"

Although the four steps are simple, that doesn't mean it's easy to liberate yourself from deeply embedded patterns of speaking and thinking. *This is a new language.*

You wouldn't expect to be able to speak French from reading one chapter in a book, and it's the same with NVC. If you wanted to learn French, it would help if you had the chance to listen to fluent speakers. You can listen to fluent NVC speakers by attending a seminar with a certified NVC trainer or by going online to enjoy a number of excellent free videos of Marshall Rosenberg teaching.

You can start your learning right away by observing the way you and the people you interact with utilize language each day. Begin to notice what happens to your energy and the energy between you and another person based on any of the four steps.

Before attempting to speak NVC, just observe what happens to your sense of connection with yourself and with someone else when you:

- make or receive an evaluation, judgment, or diagnosis.
- dish out or receive blame (including especially self-blame) or engage in speech in a manner that deflects a sense of responsibility.
- suddenly become aware of the needs that underlie your feelings or someone else's.
- make or receive a demand instead of a request.

Observe and make notes. Notice especially any tendency to judge yourself for using evaluative language. Learning NVC is a humbling and liberating process. You will accelerate your progress as you contemplate your use of language from a perspective of self-empathy, compassion, and humor. As Rosenberg counsels, "Never do anything that isn't play."

4

Transcend Fixations

Ultimately, the objective is not to just become a healthy version of your type, but to transcend the fixation, so you have a full and unfettered experience of all life has to offer.

— DENNIS PERMAN, author and expert on the Enneagram

just got off the phone with Melinda. She's in charge of engaging the keynote speaker for an event in Las Vegas that's happening three weeks from now. (That's short notice even in a world where notice is getting shorter all the time, and the timing only adds to the strong sense of urgency that is hardwired into my system.) She's calling to see if I'm available.

She apologizes for the short notice and mentions that she has just returned from maternity leave and is sorting through everything on her to-do list. I pause and tune in to the tone of her voice as she says the word *maternity*, so I ask the name of her baby. She gushes with enthusiasm as she tells me, and I ask how the name was chosen. She has two other children, ages four and seven, and I learn their names as well. Melinda and I make a real connection.

My usual habit is to get down to business, find out how many folks will be in the audience, what the theme is, the desired outcome, and so forth. Paying attention to feedback and integrating the results of various assessments, I've learned that people can perceive me as "coming on too strong" and "being too domineering." The qualities that result in these perceptions can be helpful in holding the attention of thousands of people for a ninety-minute keynote, but they aren't always as effective in other circumstances.

Through diligent self-observation and practice, asking questions and listening carefully *before* presenting my ideas have become integral aspects of my modus operandi. Now, with Melinda, I'm working on another shift out of habitual programming, practicing the art of connection by applying what various personality and social-style assessments refer to as "amiability" or "affiliative style." Amiables/Affiliatives take interest in people purely for their own sake and not as a means to an end. I make a conscious choice to take an interest in Melinda personally rather than just utilizing our conversation as a means to an end. I temporarily suspend my intense focus on securing the engagement and bring my full attention to her. I shift my attention to my heart and experience a sense of the joy she feels in motherhood. I'm discovering that being an Amiable is intrinsically rewarding.

I don't believe in astrology because I'm a Scorpio, and Scorpios are the most skeptical sign of the zodiac, but I do believe that there are two kinds of people: those who use personality profiles and those who don't. I use them, as the brief example above illustrates, to help understand and connect with myself and others.

Typological Assessments

If you work in a large organization, chances are you've already taken one or more of the contemporary typological assessments, such as the Myers-Briggs Type Indicator (MBTI), the Wilson Learning Model of Managerial Styles, the Hogan Assessments, the Personality Color Indicator (PCI), or perhaps the Enneagram Personality Profile. Typologies are valuable tools for understanding self and others. As an ENTP, Expressive/Driver, Green, Enneagram Seven (with a six wing and self-preservation subtype), I have many mirrors for reflecting on my motivations and tendencies, both when I'm alone and when interacting with others.

When I took my first personality assessment more than forty years ago (the MBTI), it was a revelation, mostly because it helped me accept and appreciate that other people see the world differently than I do. Isabel Briggs Myers (1897–1980), cocreator of the MBTI explains: "We cannot safely assume that other people's minds work on the same principles as our own. All too often, others with whom we come in contact do not reason as we reason, or do not value the things we value, or are not interested in what interests us." She articulates the purpose of learning about the different types: "By developing individual strengths, guarding against weaknesses, and appreciating the strengths of other types, life will be more amusing, more interesting, and more of a daily adventure than it could possibly be if everyone were alike."

Here are six suggestions for getting the most from typological assessments:

1. *Give up the notion that one type is better than any other.* Dr. Dennis Perman prefaces his Enneagram seminar by playfully reminding his students that "all the types suck." Perman chuckles as he explains that they suck because "they are indicative of our habitual, unconscious programming." In other words, one form of unconscious programming has no more merit than any other. Perman adds, "Your type is not a description of who you are — it's a description of where you're stuck, with clues on how to get unstuck so you can grow."

2. *Understand types, but avoid stereotyping.* One of the biggest

pitfalls in utilizing typologies is stereotyping, that is, using the language and framework of any of these systems to judge and categorize oneself or others rather than empathizing with the uniqueness underlying the predictable patterns. When people first discover the power of various typologies, they tend to see everything and everyone through the lens of that system, forgetting that each individual is unique.

In other words, as Russ Hudson, coauthor of *Discovering Your Personality Type*, emphasizes, "Our type is not our identity." He maintains that types are best understood as "default coping strategies." The challenge is to become aware of your patterns and the patterns of others without putting yourself or anyone else into a limiting box. Hudson points out:

> At different points in our lives, and even in different points in our days, we wear our type patterns more or less lightly. So there is tremendous range in the possible expression of any type, and all human beings are capable of behaviors from any of the types. Our dominant type is just that — it shows up more often than the others, but we are not confined to it. When we lose sight of this in working with others and use typing systems to reduce them to a stereotype, we can be reasonably sure that, in that moment, we are caught in the less savory parts of our own pattern and operating well below our potential.

3. *Use the insights you gain to deepen your compassion and ability to connect with others.* Many of my clients are engineers with very different personality profiles from mine. I must see the world from their point of view to communicate effectively. Therefore, I provide lots of research support for the methods and ideas I present, aiming to make a compelling, logical case, so that they feel comfortable.

When students challenge me by asking for the details of the research I cite, I don't take it as a personal attack on my credibility;

rather, I view it as a legitimate expression of their need to know. It turns out that, as I am an intuitive, enthusiastic, creative type, my growth is supported by considering my intuitions in the context of relevant, valid data.

As I learn more about the proclivities of different types, I don't take variations from the way I would do or say things as personally. When I see that people are speaking and acting based on their "wiring," it's easier to accept and to be compassionate.

4. *Use the insights you gain to deepen your compassion and ability to connect with yourself.* Just as recognizing that other people are "wired" differently makes it easier to accept and understand those differences, becoming aware of our own "wiring" — our habitual, automatic patterns of thinking, feeling, and behaving — makes it easier to be compassionate toward ourselves.

For years I criticized myself for being restless and easily bored. When I tried to learn meditation many years ago, it was almost impossible for me to sit still, and I berated myself for not being spiritually adept. As I learned more about my type, it became much easier to accept this tendency and be amused by it. The acceptance also helped me discover a creative solution: moving meditation through aikido and tai chi. As I've practiced these disciplines over the years, it's gradually become easier for me to sit still. As of this writing I've practiced a twenty-minute sitting meditation for 108 days in a row with the confident intention to continue in perpetuity.

5. *Take advantage of multiple assessments, look for cross correlations, and seek out trusted experts in interpretation.* If you take three different personality assessments and they all yield the same or complementary insights, then there's a good chance that they're accurate, especially if you're paying attention to the feedback you get from others and you discover that what you're learning from the profiles isn't unfamiliar. You can take a free version of most profiles or assessments online, but you'll get much more out of any or all of them with the benefit of a professional practitioner skilled in their use.

Over the years I've had a few tarot-card readings. Some didn't resonate, but a couple of them were astoundingly accurate. Is the accuracy of the reading a function of the type of tarot deck, the gifts of the reader, or the receptivity of the person receiving the reading?

A few years ago one of the teams I was coaching at Microsoft took the MBTI, after which we had Leslie Copland, a gifted expert, interpret the results. She sent her report, and when I handed it out to the group and we reviewed her comments on their dynamics and challenges, they were astounded at the accuracy and depth of understanding. As the leader of the group exclaimed, "She must be psychic."

Wendy Rothman is an expert in the Hogan Leadership Assessment tools. Before we began working together to design customized leadership development programs for clients based on the insights that emerge from the Hogan Assessments, I asked Wendy to do a complete assessment for me. It was remarkably accurate in both clarifying my values and highlighting my strengths as well as areas for growth. Moreover, it confirmed, clarified, and deepened the understanding I gained from Leslie's "reading." The MBTI and Hogan Assessment (and two of the tarot sessions) were complementary to the insights that have evolved over years of working with the Enneagram profile, the Wilson Learning Model of Managerial Styles, and a few others.

SUPPORTING COMPASSION, COLLABORATION, AND CONNECTION

Leslie Copland is an expert in applying a number of personality profile and typological assessment tools. I asked her to share some examples of how typologies can help teams connect and collaborate more effectively. She responded:

I was coaching a team at a global electronics company with a leader who was a classic example of the Analytical/Driver type. This type values objectivity, wants lots of data before making any decision, and then focuses relentlessly on getting things done. But the majority of people on his team were Expressive/Amiables. These folks tend to like to give and receive lots of encouragement; they're warm and like to hug their colleagues, and they make decisions primarily on intuition.

When the team members read the analysis of their types, it transformed their understanding and ability to collaborate. When they learned that their boss preferred for them to "be brief, be bold, and be gone" and not to attempt to touch or hug him without permission, they experienced a huge "Aha." Although they had intuited his discomfort with their needs for encouragement and warmth, there was something about seeing it in an objective report that allowed them to shift how they related to him. They became enthusiastic about bringing him the data he sought, striving to get to the bottom line, and recommending and carrying out action.

The best part is that as the boss read about the proclivities of his people, he started to be more attentive to the relationships and not just the tasks. He even began to share words of encouragement and the occasional hug, and the effect on the morale and effectiveness of the group was phenomenal.

Another client, the senior team at a large utility company, was almost the opposite of the electronics team. In this group the leaders were all intuitive types with grand visions about the future, but most of the staff were sensing types who could not grasp the vision without having the detailed steps to get there. The leaders said things like, "We're going to have the greatest, most successful region in the organization," and the staff would say, "And how the heck are we going to do that?" Once they learned about their different but complementary proclivities, they were able to understand and appreciate one another and do a much better job of collaborating.

Leslie emphasizes that the different typological tools she uses all make it easier for clients to be more objective about their subjectivity. She concludes, "When people read about themselves and others in the objective format of a careful typological assessment, it seems to liberate them from taking everything so personally and makes it much easier to relate with others in a way that enhances *compassion, collaboration,* and *connection."*

---

6. *Understand the most important distinction: whether you are a healthy or unhealthy version of your type.* There isn't a preferable type. All types are expressions of our habitual, default nature. But for every type there's a distinction that is qualitative and essential: Are you a healthy or unhealthy version of your type?

For example, in simple terms, I'm an archetypal Enneagram Seven, along with the following well-known characters: John Belushi, Silvio Berlusconi, Miley Cyrus, the Dalai Lama, Cameron Diaz, Robert Downey Jr., Amelia Earhart, Richard Feynman, Benjamin Franklin, Galileo Galilei, Paris Hilton, Mick Jagger, Thomas Jefferson, Sarah Palin, Joan Rivers, Charlie Sheen, Britney Spears, Steven Spielberg, Howard Stern, and Bruce Willis.

As you read through the list, you probably have a sense for the relative degree of awareness and health of each of these individuals. They're all the same type. I put them in alphabetical order, but you could probably rearrange the list in a progression from those with the weaker traits of a Seven (easily bored and distractible, gluttonous, impatient, prone to addiction, scattered, unable to make decisions) to those with healthier characteristics (creative, enthusiastic, joyous, optimistic, playful, versatile, vivacious).

Russ Hudson, cofounder of the Enneagram Institute, explains:

> The differences between healthy, average, and unhealthy expressions can be so dramatic as to seem like different types. So, for example, in the Enneagram system, healthy Eights — the most protective, constructive, and heroic of the types — can become aggressive, destructive, and vengeful as they disintegrate under stress. Healthy Ones — the most compassionate, fair-minded, and honest of people — can become cruel, intolerant, and closed-minded as they lose their center. The idea in all of our work is to discover and express the higher levels of our type, and to be more and more open to facilitating the healthiest expressions of the other types as well.

Whatever type you may be, study the characteristics of that type on the continuum from uncentered, disintegrated, and unhealthy to centered, integrated, and healthy.

As you become a more centered, integrated, and healthy version of yourself, you expand your self-knowledge and awareness, so you'll be empowered to take the next step, which is to cultivate versatility.

Cultivating Versatility

> Depending on the circumstance, you should be hard
> as a diamond, flexible as a willow, smooth-flowing
> like water, or as empty as space.
> — MORIHEI UESHIBA (1883–1969), founder of aikido

Kevin Durant, of the Oklahoma City Thunder, made headline news when he exercised his option to change teams and move to the

Golden State Warriors. ESPN's *SportsCenter* showed some of his highlight clips, including an amazing steal followed by a crossover dribble and reverse layup. At six foot eleven, Durant is the prototype of the new generation of professional basketball player who transcends the categories or positions that existed when I grew up playing the game. Now players are able to do almost anything. This exceptional versatility isn't just a priority on the court; it's becoming more important in the world of work as well.

Contemporary leaders need to be able to move freely between different modalities and styles in order to connect effectively with an increasingly diverse workforce. As we gain awareness of our own tendencies and preferences, we can become more sensitive and attuned to the preferences and sensitivities of others. When the skill of discerning the best way to communicate in order to build trust and inspire confidence is distributed throughout an organization, it contributes to *shared consciousness* and greater overall effectiveness.

Versatile Leadership That Gets Results

I'm like a box of Crayola Crayons. I see what color is needed
with different guests. This table is just plain black.
Here I need rosy pink. I draw from my palette to connect
with different guests to meet their needs.
— QUANNAH LEE, kung fu instructor,
on what it takes to be a good waiter

In his classic *Harvard Business Review* article "Leadership That Gets Results," Daniel Goleman shared important conclusions about the relative effectiveness of six different leadership styles. Working with the consulting firm of Hay-McBer, Goleman reports on a survey of more than three thousand executives and their direct subordinates from a wide range of industries aiming to determine the effect of these six leadership styles on the culture or climate of the organization. They also measured the effect of culture on financial return.

Goleman concludes that leadership style has a profound effect on the culture of the organization, and culture has a significant effect on financial returns (± 30 percent). Although four of the styles have long-term positive effects on culture and two of them have negative effects, there's a time and place for each one, and leaders need the ability to utilize them all as required.

Here's an overview of the six styles, with a brief description, the core belief or assumption that underlies each one, when to use it, its net effect on the culture of the organization, and if it's net positive, what happens when it's misused:

1. DEMOCRATIC/FACILITATIVE: Seeking the participation and contribution of all members of a team.

   CORE VABE: Everyone has something of value to offer.

   WHEN TO USE IT: When new ideas are required and engagement needs to be encouraged.

   NET EFFECT: Positive, because people feel included and valued, and new ideas are shared and developed.

   WHEN IT'S MISUSED: Results in an overemphasis on finding consensus, or a lack of direction and decisiveness.

2. AFFILIATIVE/THERAPIST: Connecting with and nurturing others emotionally.

   CORE VABE: People's feelings and well-being come first.

   WHEN TO USE IT: When morale needs to be raised or trust needs to be restored.

   NET EFFECT: Positive, because people feel cared for and respected.

   WHEN IT'S MISUSED: Results in a tendency to coddle poor performance and avoid difficult conversations about accountability.

3. AUTHORITATIVE/VISIONARY: Sharing an inspiring vision and empowering others to achieve it.

   CORE VABE: People can do great things when you help them discover the things that are worth doing.

   WHEN TO USE IT: After being Democratic and Affiliative.

   NET EFFECT: Positive, because people feel inspired and challenged.

   WHEN IT'S MISUSED: Results in lack of buy-in when used by a leader less experienced than the people being led, or a mismatch between the people's and the leader's ideas of what's worth doing and why.

4. COACHING/MENTORING: Developing people for the long term.

   CORE VABE: People can grow and learn to become more effective.

   WHEN TO USE IT: When new skills and mindsets are need to achieve organizational goals.

   NET EFFECT: Positive, because people feel that their development is valued and encouraged.

   WHEN IT'S MISUSED: May cause people to feel they are being micromanaged.

5. PACESETTER/DRIVER: Driving others toward results directly by setting high standards and carefully monitoring performance.

   CORE VABE: "If you want something done right, do it yourself."

   WHEN TO USE IT: With a small group of other self-motivated, high achievers (i.e., other Pacesetters).

   NET EFFECT: Negative, because people who aren't Pacesetters themselves feel that they can't keep up with the demands.

6. COERCIVE/COMMANDING: Telling others what to do and articulating consequences for noncompliance.

CORE VABE: "I know best."

WHEN TO USE IT: When dramatic change is necessary or in an emergency or crisis.

NET EFFECT: Negative, because people feel objectified, alienated, and disempowered.

When Goleman first reported on this research, the Authoritative/Visionary style had the strongest net positive effect on culture. Since then, there's been a shift and the Democratic/Facilitative style is becoming increasingly important.

How do you know which style you use most? If it's not intuitively obvious, you can take an assessment, but the simplest thing to do is to ask the people around you. If they're afraid to say anything, then you're probably a Pacesetter or Coercive.

Increasing diversity means that leaders need versatility — to be able to move fluidly between Visionary, Coaching, Affiliative, and Democratic styles, keeping the Pacesetter and Commanding modalities in reserve to be used judiciously.

A Versatile Leader with the Common Touch

Dennis Mannion is a remarkably versatile leader. He holds the rare distinction of having high-level executive experience in all four professional major-league sports: MLB, NHL, NBA, and NFL. Former CEO of the Detroit Pistons, he has served as president of the Los Angeles Dodgers, senior vice president of business ventures with the Baltimore Ravens, and managing director at Ascent Sports, owners of the NBA's Denver Nuggets and the NHL's Colorado Avalanche.

His leadership generates real results. For example, he helped the 2009 Dodgers lead Major League Baseball in paid attendance for the first time since 1986, and between 2011 and 2016 he brought the

Pistons from a below-average ranking to number one in the NBA in fan engagement.

When I visited the Pistons facility and walked around with Mannion, I was impressed with the way he greeted each person we encountered by name. Dennis is a master of the HQC. He remembers something personal about everyone: "How did your son do in that Little League championship game last week?" "How was that vacation in the Caribbean?"

During each interaction I watched as the faces lit up and the energy level rose as a result of his "common touch." During this visit I spent three hours with the head of Human Resources, who told me that he moved his family across the country for the opportunity to work with Dennis, because he loves to be part of a positive culture.

Dennis conveys a genuine sense of concern and creates a real connection with everyone. He also offers regular feedback to his key people, and he's open to receiving it himself. One of his assistants told me, "Dennis is an amazing coach! I love working for him, because I get the sense that he cares, and I'm getting the guidance I need to get to the next level." Dennis's strongest style, however, is Visionary. He crafted an impressive organizational charter with an inspiring vision, mission, and value statement integrated with a detailed strategic plan. He utilized the Democratic style to solicit people's ideas in crafting it and led a series of inspiring meetings to generate buy-in and support for the charter and the strategy.

When asked if he ever needs to be a Pacesetter or Coercive, he responded: "Being a Pacesetter is part of the job. The key is to not overdo it! I've got to set the right motivational tone. I push myself, and I push my people. They know they're being held accountable, but it works because they've been included in the process of setting the goals they're being pushed to achieve, and they know they're respected and valued." He continued:

Once I became aware of the model of the six styles, I realized that using the Visionary, Affiliative, Coaching, and Democratic styles with a Pacesetter's attention to accountability and leading by example means that I've very rarely had to use Coercive/Commanding to get things done. Mostly I've employed this mode soon after taking a new job. In reality it's often necessary to fire people who are consistent nonperformers and those who are purposefully obstructing the change that I was hired to make. In these situations using the Commanding style sets the stage for real Visionary leadership. After the initial housecleaning, I rarely need to ·give straight-out commands because people are aligned.

Dennis concluded: "It's important to develop the flexibility to employ all the styles in the right dosage, in an appropriate way, and at the right time. Different people need different approaches at different times! If you use only one, even a positive one, the results are deadly."

The Greatest Point of Leverage

DO THE OPPOSITE (THE COSTANZA PRINCIPLE).

Contraria sunt complementa ("Opposites are complementary").
— MOTTO OF NIELS BOHR (1885–1962),
Nobel Laureate in Physics

Although there are many different personality types, we've emphasized that one isn't better than any other. There is, however, for each personality type a fundamental and critically important distinction: *healthy* or *unhealthy*. Awake or asleep, fixed or static, flexible or rigid — whatever type you are, the most important thing is that you are becoming a healthier version of that type.

If with regard to your most important internal distinction, between healthy and unhealthy, you want to be moving toward health
and wholeness, so also in your most important external distinction,
whether you are considered *friend* or *foe*, you will want to be moving toward the positive end of the spectrum. When people meet you
they automatically, instantaneously assess you according to the basic
distinction between friend and foe. The most effective leaders in all
walks of life are able to consistently send messages that affirm *friend*,
thereby creating and reinforcing the connections that build trust,
alignment, and collaboration.

And there's one other profoundly important distinction that
is the raison d'être for this book: *skilled* or *unskilled*. If you desire
greater health and integration and want to learn how to consistently
send messages to others, verbally and nonverbally, that strengthen
the sense of connection, then practice the skills.

The essential point of leverage for developing the skill of versatility is inspired by a classic *Seinfeld* episode entitled "The Opposite." George returns from the beach and decides that every decision
that he has ever made has been wrong and that his life is the exact
opposite of what it should be. George tells this to Jerry in Monk's
Cafe, and Jerry agrees, "If every instinct you have is wrong, then
the opposite would have to be right."

George resolves to start doing the complete opposite of what he
would normally do. He orders the opposite of his normal lunch, and
he introduces himself to a beautiful woman who happens to order
exactly the same lunch, saying, "My name is George. I'm unem-
ployed, and I live with my parents." To his surprise, she is impressed
and agrees to date him. The concept for this plotline was introduced
in the pilot episode of *Seinfeld* when George tells Jerry not to clean
his bathroom before a woman visits, because "in these matters
you never do what your instincts tell you. Always, *always* do the
opposite."

Do the opposite is a humorous reference to a serious issue in developing your skills as a leader. We all have habitual patterns, default social styles, and preprogrammed tendencies. As we learn more about those patterns through typological assessments, feedback, and self-observation, we are presented with the possibility of conscious change and evolution. The nondominant and undeveloped aspects of the self are known in Jungian psychology as "inferior functions." According to Jungian analyst Marie-Louise von Franz, many people discover "that the realm of their inferior function is where they are emotional, touchy,...and they therefore acquire the habit of covering up this part of their personality." She illustrates:

> For instance, a thinking type often cannot express his feelings normally and in the appropriate manner at the right time. It can happen that when he hears that the husband of a friend has died he cries, but when he meets the widow not a word of pity will come out. [Thinking types] not only look very cold, but they really do not feel anything! They had all the feeling before, when at home, but now in the appropriate situation they cannot pull it out. Thinking types are very often looked on by other people as having no feeling; this is absolutely not true. It is not that they have no feeling, but that they cannot express it at the appropriate moment.

So, for example, thinking types have a wonderful opportunity for growth as they embrace the unknown territory of feeling and strive to express feelings in appropriate ways. And feeling types must learn to cultivate their capacity to be objective and data-oriented when appropriate.

I'm an extrovert. I get energy from being with others. I can give a keynote to an auditorium full of people and have more energy afterward than when I started. My type gets bored very easily and tends to like lots of stimuli, variety, and amusement. My habit and wiring lead me to avoid being alone and quiet. So I practice being alone and quiet. Sometimes this is incredibly difficult, just as it might be challenging for an introvert to go to a networking event. But this is how we grow.

Keith McFarland explains how he put the Costanza Principle in play:

> I was the CEO of a technology company, and we were in the midst of a huge crisis. I had ninety days to save the company. Under that kind of pressure I've observed that I revert to my core type, which you could probably describe as a blend of Authoritative, Driver, and Expressive.
>
> But I realized that if we were going to get through the challenge successfully, I would need to engage my entire senior team. I realized, with the help of 360-degree feedback, that I needed to be more receptive, more Democratic. This Democratic style is the opposite of my natural tendency!
>
> So I literally set an alarm to go off in the middle of meetings thirty minutes after we started. When the alarm went off, I would wait until whoever was speaking was finished, and then I would just go around the table and ask each person for their ideas.
>
> Nobody seemed to mind the artificial way I made myself shift to the more Democratic style. Everyone got much more engaged as a result of my questions. It was a tremendous learning experience for me. And together we saved the company!

So identify your strongest personality trait, and do the opposite!

5 Balance Energy Exchange

When we quit thinking primarily about ourselves and our own self-preservation, we undergo a truly heroic transformation of consciousness.

— JOSEPH CAMPBELL (1904–87), author of *The Power of Myth*

In late December 2004, after I had been single for seven years, I met a beautiful young opera singer at an Alexander Technique seminar in Santa Barbara, California. We made a delightful connection, but our age difference (twenty-three years) and the context of our meeting (a seminar in which I was one of the teachers) made me hesitant to think in romantic terms. When the seminar ended, we approached one another to say good-bye and exchanged a warm hug. I said, "Hey, if you are ever coming to the New York area, please let me know."

She responded, "Actually I will be there next month for my Carnegie Hall debut."

Without missing a beat I said, "Then please let me take you out to celebrate."

On January 23, 2005, we got together for dinner. I wasn't sure it was a date until she mentioned something that had happened while she was "getting ready for our date."

We shared a 1997 Ciacci Piccolomini Brunello di Montalcino. I knew that she had been living on a limited opera apprentice's budget and wasn't accustomed to drinking fine wine, but that didn't prevent her from describing the Brunello with inspiringly apt poetic language. I was transfixed. It was apparent that our connection was out of the ordinary.

Then she said, "Before this goes any further, there's an issue that concerns me."

She continued, "Like you, the last person I dated was older and more established than me, and I often felt a power imbalance. I'm concerned about how to maintain a sense of equality, a balance of power."

I responded, "Balance of power in a relationship is important to me too. Whatever the relative levels of success or experience, a healthy relationship requires open communication. I'm committed to the balanced exchange of the energy of love in whatever form is appropriate and to maintaining an open dialogue about the subject."

Well, this must have been the right answer, because she put her wineglass down and kissed me. We've been together since that first night. We believe that one of the keys to the success of our relationship almost thirteen years later is that we've both been vigilant about honoring the understanding we shared on our first date.

Givers, Takers, and Matchers

In any relationship, at home or at work, the balanced and harmonious exchange of energy is important. Adam Grant, professor of organizational behavior at Wharton Business School, offers an evidence-based, useful way to think about balance in relationships, whether at home or at work. Grant divides people into three categories: Givers, Takers, and Matchers.

Givers focus primarily on the needs of others. Givers' first instinct when they meet someone new is to wonder, "What could I possibly contribute that might benefit this person?" Givers are always ready to help. They share credit freely, look for opportunities to be of service, and do so without an expectation of benefit for themselves beyond the pleasure they get in helping others.

Takers focus primarily on their own needs. When meeting someone new, Takers' first instinct is to assess, "How can this person add value to my life? What can I get from this person?" Takers aim to exploit every interaction for their own profit and seek to claim credit, and turf, for themselves whenever possible.

Matchers focus on balancing the fulfillment of their own needs with fulfillment of the needs of others. Matchers calculate the exchange of energy and value in relationships and seek to maintain a dynamic balance.

In his book *Give and Take*, Grant reports on years of research into how these fundamental approaches affect our lives. He concludes:

- As you might expect, most people are Matchers.
- Takers, about 8 percent of the population, can thrive in the short term, but they ultimately don't do as well as Matchers, and some Givers.
- Givers are overrepresented at the top as well as the bottom of most success metrics. Givers often make the most productive salespeople, "those who put their customers' interests first," and they may achieve success in a number of realms. But they can also be easily exploited by Takers, entering into codependent relationships that drain their resources and energy.

- The most effective and ultimately fulfilling style is to be a Giver with some strategic Matcher competencies. These "otherish" people focus primarily on benefiting others, "but they also keep their own interests in the rearview mirror.... They will look for ways to help others that are either low cost to themselves or even high benefit to themselves."

Ironically, although Givers seem altruistic, they often find themselves less able to benefit others consistently because, as Grant explains, "My data, and research by lots of others, show that they're actually less generous because they run out of energy, they run out of time, and they lose their resources, because they basically don't take enough care of themselves."

Being "otherish" is the way to go! Matchers believe in and carefully monitor fairness and equality of energy exchange in relationships. They are offended when they witness Takers taking without giving in return. Matchers do what they can to rein in the exploitation of Takers. As Grant reports, "The data on this suggests that Matchers will often go around trying to punish [Takers], often by gossiping and spreading negative reputational information." And when Givers are successful despite their lack of boundaries, it's often due to the support of Matchers who are sensitive to fairness and who will go out of their way to help Givers get rewarded appropriately.

Cultivating wise, creative "otherishness" is an important element of the art of connection. When my future wife brought up the issue of balanced energy exchange on our very first date, she invoked an awareness that led us both to aspire toward *mutual otherishness*. We've learned that it truly is an art to maintain the balance of energy that allows us to meet each other's needs in a sustainable and joyful way.

For many Givers, the greatest point of leverage in this art is to develop the courage and skill to say no when appropriate.

Learn the Power of a Positive No

There is no meaningful "yes"
unless the individual could also have said "no."
— ROLLO MAY

Would you like to find a better balance in your relationships, but like many Givers and even some Matchers you have trouble saying no? Or do you say no in a way that exacerbates problems?

William Ury, coauthor of the negotiation classic *Getting to YES*, offers help in his book entitled *The Power of a Positive No*. Ury shows how the ability to say no is essential to managing one's energy and resources. A positive no is really a yes to a priority. Ury notes that common alternatives to a positive no fall into what he calls *accommodation* (fear leads you to say yes, but you don't mean it), *attack* (anger or resentment drives you to say no in a negative and unskillful manner), or *avoidance* (the inevitably futile attempt to ignore problems).

There are three steps to a positive no:

1. Say yes to your deeper need. Affirm that need for yourself and express it clearly.
2. Say no to what does not support your need in a respectful manner.
3. Express your intention to seek a positive outcome and offer creative ideas to get to an alternative yes.

The positive no is a critical key to focusing on and realizing your priorities. Entrepreneur and businessman Steve Jobs (1955–2011) stated, "Focusing is about saying 'no.'" When we say no to something that is not a priority, we liberate attention and energy to say yes to what's most important. Former British prime minister Tony Blair explains, "The art of leadership is saying no, not saying yes. It is very easy to say yes."

If you have trouble saying no, it's a good idea to practice, beginning with little things in everyday life; for example, practice saying no to the upsell at the restaurant: "Thanks, but I prefer my burger without the fries."

You can cultivate the art of the positive no by learning to reframe. For example, let's say you're a manager and one of your team members requests funding for executive coaching sessions. If you answer, "No, it's not in the budget" (We've all heard this one!), you risk alienating your team member. Instead, learn to respond with an affirmation and a creative challenge: "I'd like to approve funding for coaching, but we've got a limited budget. Let's explore how we might be able to find the funds."

Sam Horn, author of *Tongue Fu*, has a black belt in reframing a negative no into a positive one. She invites us to imagine this scene. You're the boss and an employee asks, "Can I have my paycheck early? I'm going to Las Vegas this weekend." You answer, "Sorry, you can't because it hasn't been approved by payroll." That's the truth; however, the employee may get upset because you're rejecting the request. The words *can't because* are like a verbal door slamming in the employee's face.

Sam counsels a more positive alternative. You can often approve requests with the words *Sure, as soon as* or *Yes, right after.* Reword your reply: "*Sure*, you can have your paycheck, *as soon as* it's approved by payroll. Why don't we give them a call, explain the circumstances, and see if there's any way they can speed things up."

The same strategy works at home. One of Sam's clients explains how he applied it:

> My kids see me as a big meanie, because they're constantly asking for permission, and I'm always telling them no. Next time they ask if they can go outside and play with their friends, instead of telling them, "No, you can't, because you haven't finished your homework," I'm going to say, "Sure

you can, *right after* you finish your homework." Instead of seeing me as the one who's keeping them from what they want, this makes them responsible for getting what they want. It changes the whole dynamic of our relationship.

The other side of this important equation is learning how to find the yes behind others' no, even if they aren't skilled at expressing it. If we can free ourselves from the tendency to judge and interpret a no as a rejection, in other words, if we can avoid taking it personally, then we may be able to discover and empathize with the needs behind the other person's unwillingness to assent. Awareness of those needs opens new possibilities for connection and creativity.

Manage Expectations: Promise Low and Deliver High

Never promise more than you can perform.

— PUBLILIUS SYRUS (85–43 BCE), Roman author

Many of our happinesses — and all of our disappointments — are a function of expectations. If you go to a Michelin three-star restaurant and it's good but not great, you'll probably be unhappy, but if you stay at an inexpensive bed and breakfast and you discover fresh flowers in your room and homemade muffins at breakfast, you will probably rave to your friends about this wonderful place. Managing expectations, for yourself and others, is a simple but profoundly important aspect of building and maintaining positive relationships.

Well-meaning folks often get enthusiastic about what they would like to be able to do for others without thinking it through. This is one of the reasons that Givers sometimes burn out; they want to please, so they overpromise and then become extremely stressed in the attempt to fulfill what they aren't able to do.

One of the pieces of wisdom given by Don Miguel Ruiz in his book *The Four Agreements* is: "Always be impeccable with your word." We all know that integrity is measured by doing what we say we are going to do. But being impeccable doesn't just mean doing what you say; it also means being extremely careful about what you say, especially what you promise.

If, for example, you call a meeting, promise people that it will be over by 4:00, and keep them until 4:30, you will not only lose some credibility, but you will also probably have a less productive meeting. You will get much better results if you tell people to plan to stay until 5:00 and that you will try to get them out earlier. Then, when the meeting ends at 4:30, you're a hero.

"When people ask me what I do for a living, I often respond that my job is all about managing expectations," explains Kevin Patterson. Patterson, a former artistic director and executive producer of opera companies in Austin, Anchorage, and Indianapolis, notes that a typical opera production comes together in as little as four weeks. He says:

> On the first day of rehearsal the singers, many of whom haven't worked together before, are introduced to a production team comprised of a director, stage manager, and conductor who themselves may not have worked together. Everyone needs to feel comfortable quickly, to create a sense of mutual trust, so they can open themselves up to the kind of creative exploration that makes a great performance. And then of course, there's the opera board, the donors, the volunteers, the costume and makeup team, and most important — the audience.
>
> My job is to ensure that everyone gets what's needed to put on an production of sublime artistic excellence that will make all the stakeholders feel fulfilled. The key to making this happen is paradoxical: I expect the best from everyone, and that includes expecting them to bring out the best in each other, and at the same time I manage expectations

carefully. I might, for example, need to gently inform the soprano before she arrives that her dressing room is smaller than the one at the Met; and I may need to let the stage director know that the budget for props is much less than the one at Covent Garden.

Then when the soprano arrives and the dressing room is small, she's actually delighted when she finds the chocolates and welcome note that await her. The director already knows what the budgetary constraints are, but when he arrives we have a talk in which I let him know that his creativity isn't subject to limitations. Connecting with people one-to-one allows me to adjust expectations and keep the energy flowing.

Software architects Raphael Malveau and Thomas Mowbray refer to this important element of relationship building and energy leadership as "perceptual engineering":

> People know that if they announce that an idea will deliver wonderful benefits, others will be dissatisfied, should their expectations not be met, and could lose confidence in the promisers' ability to produce in the future. However, using the techniques from expectation management, the promiser will carefully articulate the potential good and bad outcomes, perhaps even overemphasizing the negatives. Then... those promised will be pleasantly surprised because more was delivered than they were led to expect!

Robert Tangora is a Renaissance man who, in addition to being a tai chi master, author, and attorney, also ran a business restoring antiques in New York City for many years. Robert can strip away old layers of paint and grime on an Empire card table to reveal the beauty of the original finish or stabilize the wobbly legs and armrest of a Louis XVI chair. He comments, "People would come into my shop with all sorts of things. And, being New Yorkers, they always wanted it done 'right away.' But I understood that a large part of my business was to manage their expectations. If I thought I might be able to get a finish restored in three months, I'd usually say it would take four. When I delivered it in three and a half, they would be ecstatic."

This is another point that just seems so obvious. Of course we all know this, just as we all know how important it is to give others our full attention when we are listening. Yet when we make promises — to call people back, complete projects by certain dates, attend Little League games, show up for meetings, prepare reports, cancel reservations, and so on — and don't *do* these things, we deplete the energy that supports positive relationships. *So promise low and deliver high.*

Adjust the Balance of Energy with Feedback

I think it's very important to have a feedback loop,
where you're constantly thinking about what you've done
and how you could be doing it better.
— ELON MUSK, CEO of Tesla and SpaceX

My wife and I just celebrated our anniversary. We have been together for twelve wonderful years. Every week we go for a long walk and engage in the simple practice of taking turns sharing our thoughts and feelings about the relationship. We ask one another: "Is there anything going on that may be difficult to express?" "Is there anything I can do to be more loving and supportive?"

We ask for feedback, so that we can effectively monitor and adjust the balance of our energy exchange. We take turns responding, and we don't interrupt. Sometimes we share major issues. I learned over the course of these walks, for example, that she wanted to move back to the East Coast, but was hesitant to express this, because she knew how much I loved living in the Southwest. Other times, the issues seem smaller. I recently shared my feelings about the current state of our procedure for disposing of the copious quantities of dog doo that our two adorable Akitas manufacture on a regular basis; and I followed this with a specific actionable request ("Please don't leave the plastic bags of dog doo on top of the garbage shed. Please place them in a larger bag inside the shed.") We now live happily on the East Coast, and our garbage shed is unadorned with bags of Akita poo.

Our feedback conversations are often exchanges of gratitude and praise, but that's probably because we've been focused on mutual otherishness — eliciting, listening, and responding to one another's concerns and needs — ever since our first date.

Professionally, I discovered the value of giving and receiving feedback when I began coleading seminars with Tony Buzan, the creator of Mind Mapping. From 1979 to 1982 Tony and I traveled the world together. We went to Japan, Australia, Singapore, France, Switzerland, Sweden, and many other places, leading five-day retreats for senior managers.

At the end of every seminar we went for a long walk and gave one another feedback on how we could be more effective. We began with a self-critique and then asked for feedback on what could be improved. We agreed not to interrupt, defend, or justify, but rather to listen deeply. After focusing on what could be improved, we shared our perceptions of what was most effective and expressed appreciation. We then translated what we learned into clear, positive intentions for change.

I learned so much from this practice. Tony was sharp in his critiques, and his specific feedback helped me accelerate my development as a speaker, facilitator, and teacher. And, just as valuable, my ability to observe and give constructive feedback evolved considerably. Moreover, I internalized the process, thereby improving my ability to critique my own work, a process that continues with every presentation or class I offer.

Author and leadership expert Ken Blanchard calls feedback the "breakfast of champions." But for many people that meal is indigestible. You can make it much more palatable by understanding the paradox that most people do want information that will help them be more effective and successful, yet at the same time they want to feel that they are fine just the way they are! If you bear this paradox in mind, you'll be much more effective.

SMART Feedback

So, what are the ingredients of highly nutritious feedback, and how can you make it as appetizing as possible? Constructive feedback is SMART:

S   Specific
M   Monitored
A   Actionable
R   Respectful
T   Timely

Specific

Specifics are more constructive than generalities. To tell someone, "You are insensitive to clients," or "You are a slob," is not as useful or constructive as, "You interrupted the client twice and didn't make eye contact," or "Your shirttail was hanging out and your shoes weren't shined."

Remembering our earlier discussion about the difference between evaluation and observation will go a long way in helping you with this key to feedback. The first two examples in the previous paragraph are generalities, but they are also *evaluations*, and hence not advisable. The second two examples are more specific; they are also *observations*, which are much more effective. Focus on *what is said and done* — the actual, the concrete, the specific — *not on your opinion or interpretation*, which usually casts a wider net.

Attend to the observable rather than the inferred. And don't tell others why they did what they did (making assumptions about their motivation is evaluation). If you are unsure of someone's motivation or intent, then ask for clarification.

Monitored

The only way to measure the success of a communication is through the results you achieve. So measure your effectiveness as a giver of feedback by the changes of behavior that you observe in its wake. The *Business Dictionary* notes, "Response to a stimulus (such as criticism or praise) is considered feedback only if it brings about a change in the recipient's behavior."

Complete your feedback session by asking the recipient to express what he or she has understood. Check that the response matches your associations with your original message.

Actionable

To be useful, feedback must refer to a behavior that a person can change. To remind people of something that they are powerless to change only increases their frustration and sabotages trust; for example, "John, I'm afraid that you just aren't tall enough to cut the right figure in sales meetings." Instead, you might say, "John, let's find a way to strengthen your presence in sales meetings." Feedback is useful to the extent that it inspires people to take specific actions to improve their performance.

Respectful

For your feedback to be taken to heart, you must create and sustain a connection by creating an atmosphere of rapport, trust, and respect.

The key is to distinguish between the unchanging, soul essence of a person that is perfect as it is and the behaviors of the person that may benefit from adjustment. If your feedback springs from this awareness, then people will increasingly seek you out to ask for it.

And feedback is usually most effective when solicited rather than imposed. Before launching into a discourse on individuals' performance, it is a good idea to *ask* them to evaluate their areas for improvement first. People are usually much more receptive to your observations when you demonstrate respect by asking for theirs. Moreover, by asking first, and listening carefully, you will usually learn something valuable that you would not have known otherwise.

Timely

In December and January many organizations require their managers to give and receive annual performance reviews. This is usually a rather grim and lifeless process. When feedback is given once a year, it tends to feel onerous and irrelevant. Performance feedback is more effective when it's shared in a timely and relevant way. It works best when it's part of an organization's culture. I define culture as "the way we do things around here." And when part of that way is to share openly how we can be more effective, then there's an elevation of energy, engagement, and performance.

It seems as though it should be common sense that feedback is most useful when given promptly. If you want to give someone feedback on performance at a meeting, for example, give it as soon as possible after the meeting, when all parties are more likely to remember what happened, rather than a few weeks later when recall may be dimming.

In addition to being timely, you want to ensure that the feedback is well-timed. Sensitivity to receptiveness and emotional state is key. Ask, "Is this a good time for me to give you some feedback on your performance?" or "When can we get together for a feedback session?" The best feedback is useless if the time or place prevents it from being digested. For example, even the most brilliant critical feedback will almost always do more harm than good if offered in public.

Giving and receiving feedback in an open and supportive fashion creates a positive leadership culture. It is a core competency that allows us to, as Sisodia and his colleagues advise in *Firms of Endearment*, create partner relationships that really are mutually beneficial.

It's an art that requires attention and practice — and tact.

The Lost Art of Tact

Honesty is not greater where elegance is less.

— SAMUEL JOHNSON (1709–84),
British poet, essayist, and literary critic

When a person says, "Let me be brutally honest," or "No offense, but…," chances are someone is about to be brutalized or offended. Honesty doesn't require that we blurt out everything at any time just because it happens to be true. Elegance and diplomacy are essential to the art of connection. Whimsically defined as "the ability to tell someone to go to hell in such a way that they look forward to the trip," tact is the skill of sharing awkward information in a way that others can hear and integrate.

Although some managers offer feedback that is tactless, brutal, and judgmental, it is equally common to err by trying too hard to be nice. Nonperformers are frequently coddled and given positive reviews, because the manager in charge doesn't want to hurt anyone's feelings or take responsibility for writing an unsatisfactory evaluation. Paradoxically, being too nice is a grave insult. The underlying message is that persons treated this way are incapable of learning, growing, and improving their performance.

Moreover, if you can't find areas of improvement for your people to work on, then you shouldn't be a manager and you will never be a leader. Leaders find the courage to tell people the truth even when it isn't comfortable. When offering constructive feedback, avoid sugarcoating. Tell people when you are not satisfied with their performance and specifically why. Guide them to create a plan for change. Encourage them to do their best.

Tact in Difficult Conversations

Hendrie "Hank" Weisinger is the author of *Performing Under Pressure*, *The Power of Positive Criticism*, and many other books. An expert on "how to give and take criticism," Hank is renowned for coaching leaders to excel in "difficult conversations." I asked Hank about a challenging scenario that most of us would dread: "How do you criticize a colleague at work for lack of personal hygiene? In other words, is there a tactful way to tell someone, 'You stink!'?"

Hank muses, "Most people break out in a sweat at the thought. If you follow three steps, you still may perspire while giving the criticism, but what you say won't stink."

Step one is to understand what makes it difficult to tell someone he or she smells. It's embarrassing! Most people report that a situation like this is so mortifying that they'd rather live with the offensive odor than risk communication about it.

How can we manage the embarrassment? The key is to be aware of and acknowledge it. The simplest way to acknowledge that you are embarrassed is to say, "I feel embarrassed bringing this up." You will find that expressing the feeling of embarrassment reduces the tension of the situation immediately.

Step two is to begin in a way that demonstrates respect and protects the person's self-esteem. A tactful way is to mention the criticized behavior as if the individual is unaware of it; if the person is not aware, there is no reason to be embarrassed. Even if she is aware of her offensive odor, she can now save face by thanking you for something that she "was not aware of." "I'll take care of it immediately" is the usual response.

One of the concerns in giving this type of criticism is that it is too personal and not work-related. Hank explains that the third step is to make the criticism work-related by explaining how improving the personal hygiene issue will enhance the workplace, so it's clear that it's a performance issue, not a personal one.

I asked Hank to put the three steps together, so we can learn what a tactful approach might sound like.

He responded: "You might say: 'I'm embarrassed I have to tell you this, and I'm sure you may be embarrassed too; nevertheless, it's important. You are probably not aware that people in the office have mentioned that you have some body odor, and it's making it difficult for some clients and coworkers to work closely with you. I thought you'd want me to bring it to your attention, so you could take care of the matter.'"

Hank emphasizes that this approach doesn't magically make difficult conversations easy. But he agrees that if we connect first with ourselves by acknowledging our own feelings — in this example, embarrassment — and then connect with others by sharing information in a respectful and compassionate manner, we greatly enhance the likelihood of positive outcomes while building healthier relationships.

The Art of Praise

You can tell the character of every man
when you see how he gives and receives praise.
— SENECA (4 BCE–65 CE), Roman Stoic philosopher

Learning to give and receive constructive criticism and feedback skillfully, especially in embarrassing or difficult situations, is an important skill for monitoring and adjusting the balance of energy exchange. It's challenging and takes lots of practice. It's just as important to develop your skill in giving and receiving praise.

In *The One Minute Manager*, Kenneth Blanchard and Spencer Johnson popularized the notion of "catching people doing something right." Chances are, according to their research, most people in your organization and family feel underappreciated. They found that, to be perceived as evenhanded, you must give four positive comments for every negative one.

Ken explains, "People who feel good about themselves produce good results, and people who produce good results feel good about themselves." In other words, well-delivered praise fuels the positive cycle of energy exchange in relationships and deepens the sense of trust and connection.

PRAISE is an acronym to help you remember how to generate good feelings and positive connection.

PRAISE

P   Precise
R   Relevant
A   Amiable
I   Inspiring
S   Sincere
E   Encouraging

Precise

> Nothing is more effective than sincere, accurate praise,
> and nothing is more lame than a cookie-cutter compliment.
> — BILL WALSH (1931–2004), American football coach

Generic comments like "Way to go," "You aced that presentation," or "Awesome, Dawg" may communicate that you're pleased with someone's performance, but your praise will create more good feeling and connection if you can articulate it more precisely. For example, you can share the specific observations that led you to the conclusion that a colleague "aced" a presentation. What new insights did you gain from the presentation? What aspects of the delivery did you experience as most compelling? What feelings were evoked and what needs of yours were met by the presentation?

Relevant

> You do ill if you praise...in a matter you do not understand.
> — LEONARDO DA VINCI

The word *relevant* is derived from the Latin *relevare*, meaning "to raise up." Your praise will be uplifting if it's appropriate to the situation or behavior. Author Pearl S. Buck cautions, "Praise out of season, or tactlessly bestowed, can freeze the heart as much as blame." For example, although in a social setting a compliment about hairstyle, clothing, or appearance might be just right, in a professional setting it can have the opposite effect.

Amiable

> The love of praise, however concealed by art,
> Reigns more or less, and glows in every heart.
> — EDWARD YOUNG (1683–1765), English poet

One of the secrets of praising for maximum positive effect is to adopt the style of an Amiable or Affiliative when you do it. (Amiables and Affiliatives value others for their own sake. They believe that people are the first priority.) In other words, avoid the tendency to utilize praise as a "carrot" to attempt to reward, reinforce, or "motivate" people toward a particular end. The most effective praise — with regard to creating genuinely positive feelings and deeper connection

— is shared as something of intrinsic value, a pure celebration of another person's accomplishment, achievement, or effort.

Inspiring

> There are two things people want more than sex and money...
> recognition and praise.
>
> — MARY KAY ASH (1918–2001), legendary entrepreneur

Paradoxically, when praise is delivered as a celebration in truly amiable fashion rather than as a "motivational technique," it is genuinely inspiring — and not just to the person who receives it. When you catch someone doing something right and celebrate it, you'll discover that you're multiplying the joy in your own life.

Christine Ranck, the author of *Ignite the Genius Within*, who as we learned in Chapter 2 managed to bring out the best in her apartment superintendent, also shared an interaction she had recently with a customer representative from her telecom provider. Chris had been overcharged. She contacted the customer-service department and was delighted when her problem was resolved in a timely and courteous manner. Chris wrote a note praising the person who helped her. Here's the note she received a couple of weeks later:

> My boss received your comments today and called me into his office. I thought I had done something wrong. Instead he showed me your letter and thanked me for doing a good job. He said to keep it up and that he would write a recommendation for a salary increase. Your letter made me cry. Hardly anyone ever bothers to write about their service with us. I feel lucky to have answered your phone call. Thank you so much for taking the trouble. It has really helped me and made me feel really good.

Chris comments, "I'm always looking for the best in others and aiming to acknowledge it. This is a wonderful source of joy and inspiration in my life."

Sincere

> You must go on trying to be sincere. Each day you put on a mask, and you must take it off little by little.
> — G. I. GURDJIEFF (1866–1949), author of
> *Life Is Real Only Then, When "I Am"*

When people dole out compliments as part of their repertoire of politeness, they dilute and distort the power of praise. Most people can discern the difference between organic honey and high-fructose corn syrup. Insincere praise, or "damning with faint praise," can be alienating and disconnecting.

It's possible to be polite and tactful *and* genuine and sincere. In other words, sincerity doesn't mean you should say everything that comes to mind, but rather that you should be mindful and mean everything you do say. Sincerity is a rare and precious quality predicated on openness and humility.

Encouraging

> My mother's words became the theme of my childhood. They've stayed with me all my life. "You can do it."
> — MARY KAY ASH

When praise is precise, relevant, amiable, inspiring, and sincere, it will always be encouraging, but praise is different from encouragement. Praise focuses on specific aspects of a person's performance or behavior, whereas encouragement is a more general statement about one's belief in the core capacity of another.

Encourage means "to inspire with courage, spirit, or hope." Classic encouraging phrases include:

"I know you can do it."

"I'm sure you can find a way."

"I believe in you."

Sometimes it's more useful to offer critical feedback than it is to offer praise. Other times praise is just right. But encouragement is almost always well received.

Receiving Praise

Appropriate praise is a gift of energy. Yet when it comes to receiving praise, people have developed many strategies to deflect or minimize it: "It's nothing," "*De rien,*" "*De nada.*"

Instead of dismissing or deflecting praise, accept it graciously. Allow yourself to be moved by expressions of gratitude. Avoid false humility and inflated pomposity. Say "Thank you," "*Merci beaucoup,*" "*Muchas gracias.*"

You can also help others deliver their praise in a way that will enrich the experience for both the giver and the receiver. In other words, asking someone to be more precise after a compliment can often lead to dialogue that is more relevant or useful.

For example, here's a dialogue that took place after a recent keynote speech:

STUDENT: You're the greatest speaker I've ever heard!

SPEAKER: Thank you. May I ask what inspired you to share that delightful observation?

STUDENT: What do you mean?

SPEAKER: How did the presentation affect you to lead you to that conclusion?

STUDENT: I don't know. It was just so inspiring.

SPEAKER: Was there something in particular that inspired you?

STUDENT: Well, yeah, actually. When you said that genius is our birthright, that every healthy child is born with abundant curiosity, imagination, and energy. I realized that these qualities might still be there within me, and I felt a surge of hope.

SPEAKER: And did that feeling of hopefulness come out of something you feel you needed?

STUDENT: Yes! I've been needing encouragement. I've been getting so many discouraging messages lately, every time I turn on the television, and at work too.

SPEAKER: So you thought the presentation was great because it touched you in a way that gives you hope and encouragement?

STUDENT: Exactly!

SPEAKER: Well, thank you for telling me. I feel more hopeful and encouraged when people resonate with the message of hope and encouragement.

SMART feedback and PRAISE are important skills that leaders need to balance energy exchange. Mutual otherishness works when we are continually improving our ability to understand and meet one another's needs, and sharing feedback constructively helps us do that more efficiently and effectively. As you learn to seek feedback, you sharpen your ability to meet other people's needs. As you learn to give it, you support others in meeting your needs with greater efficiency and effectiveness. This positive loop of feedback builds trust, alignment, and connection.

SMART Feedback Becomes More Important as You Gain Power

Leaders know the importance of having someone in their lives
who will unfailingly and fearlessly tell them the truth.

— WARREN BENNIS

Every day there seems to be a news story about a powerful person
who has been arrested for corruption. Why do so many people become corrupt as they assume power? Character is like a vessel, and
power is like wine. As the vessel is filled with increasing amounts
of wine, the tiny cracks in it start to appear. (Some people have obvious, gaping holes in their character; but everyone has these tiny
cracks. People who claim to have perfect vessels are delusional.) To
avoid becoming drunk with power, leaders must recognize that *as
they achieve success, feedback becomes more important.* If you are surrounded by people who always agree with you, something is wrong.
If you believe all of your own publicity, you are headed for a fall.

As organizations strive to become more collaborative and develop shared consciousness, free-flowing SMART feedback becomes more important, at all levels. In the early days of my career,
C-level executives often acted as though they didn't need feedback
(or training). This has been changing rapidly.

Renowned executive coach Marshall Goldsmith, author of
Triggers, reports: "When I became an executive coach, few CEOs
received feedback from their colleagues. Even fewer candidly discussed that feedback and their personal developmental plans with
anyone. Today, many of the world's most respected chief executives
are setting a positive example by opening up, striving continually to
develop themselves as leaders."

Goldsmith cites the example of former General Mills CEO
Steve Sanger, who opened up in a meeting with his extended executive team: "Last year my team told me that I needed to do a better
job of coaching those who reported directly to me. I just reviewed

my 360-degree feedback. I have been working on becoming a better coach for the past year or so. I'm still not doing quite as well as I want, but I'm getting a lot better. My coworkers have been helping me improve. Another thing that I feel good about is the fact that my scores on 'Effectively responds to feedback' are so high this year."

When a leader like Sanger demonstrates this kind of humility and curiosity about how to improve, it sets a positive example encouraging people at all levels of the organization to be more open to the free flow of feedback. In an interview with *USA Today*, Sanger noted that when he got his MBA at the University of Michigan Ross School of Business, he learned that humility was the key to leadership. After retiring he and his wife donated $20 million to the school to expand leadership development programs with the aim of "developing leaders who make a positive difference in the world."

In Chapter 1 we learned that one of the definitions of humility is "a manifested willingness to view oneself accurately." Seeking feedback is evidence of that willingness.

The Greatest Point of Leverage

CULTIVATE MUTUAL OTHERISHNESS.

Who is the happiest of men? He who values the merits of others, and in their pleasure takes joy, even as though 'twere his own.
— JOHANN WOLFGANG VON GOETHE

Heaven and hell are set up the same way. In each place people sit at large rectangular banquet tables. The tables are set beautifully and replete with every imaginable delicacy. All the diners in both settings have large wooden paddles strapped to their hands, and the paddles can't be removed. In hell all the diners are Takers who try to feed themselves, food flies in all directions, and fights break out constantly. In heaven all the diners are *otherish* and feed those across from them at the table.

How can you cultivate a more heavenly world of mutual otherishness?

First, go to www.adamgrant.net/selfgivertaker and do the free self-assessment, so you can better understand your current default setting. (There's also a free 360-degree assessment, where you can get other people to rate you.) Many people discover that they are Takers in some circumstances, for example, when bargaining over the price of a car, and Givers or Matchers in other instances, for example, when a friend needs a favor or a colleague needs advice. Grant's assessment will help you discern your fundamental style.

Once you've assessed yourself, make it a practice to assess whether a person you are tempted to help is a Taker, a Giver, or a Matcher. If you determine that someone is a Taker, be more measured and careful in what and how much you give.

Think creatively about how you can provide the greatest benefit for others with the minimum effort. Grant suggests that you ask yourself: "What are the types of giving that I find most energizing or that are most consistent with my skills?"

Master the art of the "five-minute favor." Grant advocates strategic generosity, giving to others in a way that doesn't deplete our own resources and energy. He proposes, for example, that we make it a habit to consider, on a daily basis, how we can best provide support to others in five minutes or less. It can be as simple as introducing people to those who can help them, retweeting the tweets of those you follow, or penning handwritten notes of appreciation.

If you cultivate otherishness in these ways, you'll become more of a glowworm. Formulate the intention to attract more otherish people into your life, and be wary and judicious in your dealings with Takers. Whether at work or at home, the most harmonious, enlivening exchange of energy emerges when all parties in a relationship are focused on meeting one another's needs in efficient and creative ways.

Now, since the best people are more aware of their options and possibilities than ever before, organizations that develop and sustain cultures based on mutual otherishness will do a much better job of attracting and retaining high-performance talent. Mutual otherishness is another way of expressing the fundamental new rule introduced in *Firms of Endearment*: "Create partner relationships that really are mutually beneficial."

In the past most people didn't know it was possible to make a positive difference in the world — and be successful — by looking after the welfare of all the stakeholders in an enterprise. But now that we do know, why would you consider doing anything else?

6

Be a RARE Listener

Everything that needs to be said has already been said. But since no one was listening, everything must be said again.

— ANDRÉ GIDE (1869-1951), Nobel Laureate in Literature

E very book, blog, and Linked-In post on leadership, parenting, relationships, or emotional intelligence has something to offer about the importance of listening and how to improve this critical leadership competency. Even if, in spite of Gide's quip, you *have* been listening, let's consider how to improve this essential relationship-building skill.

Listening Is like Driving

Ever notice that anyone going slower than you is an idiot,
but anyone going faster is a maniac?
— GEORGE CARLIN (1937–2008), humorist

My friends in Los Angeles swear that the worst drivers in the country are to be found on the 405, but anyone from DC will tell you they're on the Beltway. Folks from New Jersey commiserate about the Turnpike, but Bostonians will tell you that the Callahan Tunnel is the epicenter of bad driving. If you speak with Italians, Brazilians, or Indians, they'll explain that the standard of driving in their countries makes U.S. drivers look tame. Yet, although people are quick to agree that the general standard of driving leaves much to be desired, most people believe that they are above-average drivers.

Listening is like driving — most people think they are better than average, but that can't be true.

THE DUNNING-KRUGER EFFECT

In a classic study entitled "Unskilled and Unaware of It: How Difficulties in Recognizing One's Own Incompetence Lead to Inflated Self-Assessments," psychologists Justin Kruger and David Dunning report that in many social and intellectual domains "people who lack the knowledge or wisdom to perform well are often unaware of this fact." Dunning and Kruger's subjects overestimated their prowess in logical reasoning, grammar, and sense of humor.

Researchers at the University of Stockholm in Sweden posed the question: "Are we all less risky and more skillful than our fellow drivers?" The answer? No! Other studies have found that people often overestimate their popularity, job performance, and relationship abilities.

Bad driving is common, and so is bad listening. Before we explore the art of listening well, let's consider the everyday manifestations of bad listening.

How do you know when someone isn't listening? Let us count the ways!

Think back over your last week:

Have you had people check their messages or text while you were trying to speak to them?

Have you been interrupted?

Has anyone fidgeted, checked his watch, or rolled his eyes at you?

Have you had someone fail to make eye contact, look at her device, or change the subject when you were speaking?

Professor Sherry Turkle reports that 89 percent of Americans admit they took out a phone at their last social encounter — and 82 percent say that they felt the conversation deteriorated after they did so.

And just as you may have been cut off by someone in a rush to get to work or stuck behind a torturously slow car in the fast lane, chances are that at some point another driver felt that you cut him off or that you failed to signal before turning. As you reflect on the bad listening manifestations that you've observed in others, please consider the possibility that others may have perceived you as being a less than ideal listener.

A Bad-Listening Exercise

Take an inventory of your relationships and contemplate with humility and curiosity how you can become a better listener. You can deepen your insight and have some fun by experimenting with the following listening exercise.

For this exercise, you'll need a partner. Tell your partner about something that interests you. Choose a topic that is meaningful, something that you'd really like to share. You might, for example, offer your thoughts on a political issue, ideas for a vacation you're planning, or memories from the best concert you ever attended. Your partner's job is to practice bad listening — to manifest as many nonaffirming listening habits as possible. Your task is to persist in communicating your message. After a minute or so, switch roles. Aim to do a worse job of listening than your partner did.

When this exercise is practiced in a class setting, the results are always fascinating. Tension quickly fills the room, often manifested in near hysterical laughter. Even though everyone knows it's only a game, the stress generated is palpable. The result is that participants become sensitized to the manifestations of bad listening. This sets the stage for a deeper consideration of listening.

The Key to Shared Consciousness

What if I told you that you had a magical superpower that could transform your relationships while enriching your life dramatically? You have the power. It's called empathy.

Legendary Duke basketball coach Mike Krzyzewski explains: "As a coach, a parent, or a leader of any kind, one of the most important things that you can feel for one of your 'teammates' is empathy. If someone believes that you can identify with their situation and understand their feelings, they are more apt to trust you, which leads to faster responses to situations and better conclusions."

Empathy is the key to mutual otherishness and shared consciousness. The word comes from the Greek root *empatheia*, meaning "affection, passion." It's at the heart of the art of connection.

In colloquial language, we speak about putting ourselves in someone else's position. Some guides to listening actually teach this as a technique. They encourage you to assume the posture of the person to whom you're listening as a way to establish rapport. It's much more effective, however, to really open yourself to the feeling of rapport by giving your full attention to the other person. Your body language will then align with the speaker's in a natural and authentic way.

Public radio host and conversation expert Celeste Headlee advises: "Many of you have already heard a lot of advice on this, things like look the person in the eye,...look, nod, and smile to show that you're paying attention. I want you to forget all of that. It is crap. There is no reason to learn how to show you're paying attention if you are in fact paying attention."

THE AL RULE

Keith McFarland is a legendary character, and I was keen to meet him and interview him for this book. When I discovered that we would both be presenting at an executive summit in Houston, I stalked him (constructively) by arriving early to attend his talk and by asking the host to introduce us.

My immediate impression was that the folksy, engaging, and unpretentious style of his presentation wasn't an act — this was the real person. I felt that he gave me his full attention, and he expressed what I experienced as genuine enthusiasm for getting to know me and contributing to this book. This inspired my curiosity. Did his gift for connecting with people come naturally, or was it something he learned?

During our interview we talked for hours, and the time disappeared. He told me that one doesn't become a business school dean at age twenty-six without being a very driven, achievement-oriented person. In the middle of his stratospheric rise he experienced a minor nervous breakdown and started to feel depressed despite his accomplishments.

I asked him about the lessons he learned from this challenging time in his life, and he responded, "Let me tell you about the Al Rule." Keith explains:

I found my way to a therapist named Al, and I credit him for putting me on a path to the life I have today. The help he gave me wasn't a function of some exceptional insight into my childhood or analysis of the motives of my behavior; it was the simple experience of his presence. He was able to just be there and listen to me. I felt that he accepted me fully, just as I was, and that I could always call him, that he would always be there if I needed him.

Al's ability to be fully present with me changed my life. Not only did I recover from my depression, but I decided that for the rest of my life I would invoke what I call the "Al Rule." The Al Rule is to meet people where they are and to be as present with them as I can be, to listen with care, patience, and kindness every chance I get.

Keith is in demand around the world and his strategic advisory business is booked years in advance with an overflow of clients. I asked him how he remembers to apply the Al Rule in the midst of all of this.

He chuckled and said: "My thirteen-year-old Australian cattle dog is my main teacher now. I can be up and down, but he's always the same. His presence gives me feedback on how I'm doing. I just have to remember to pet him every time I come home. My dog keeps me centered!"

"Be My Girlfriend"

I learned an important lesson about empathy and the art of connection many years ago. My friend Alice was having a rough time. Her marriage had fallen apart and she was involved in a painful divorce, she had just been diagnosed with a melanoma, and she was going through a difficult professional transition as well. We made arrangements to get together for dinner. The first thing she said to me when I arrived was, "I need you to be my girlfriend this evening."

"Excuse me?" I replied.

"No, really. I do need you to be more like a girlfriend this evening," Alice said. "I'm really hurting. I'm frightened and discouraged. All of my guy friends are trying to give me advice to help me deal with this mess that is my life. Right now, I don't want any advice. I just need you to be present with me and listen, more like what my best female friend does for me. Do you think that's something you can do?"

I agreed. It wasn't easy. My mind wandered. I wanted to make jokes to ease the tension. But instead I chose to be quiet and just be with her as deeply as possible.

At the end of the evening Alice gave me a big hug and thanked me enthusiastically. She called me the next day to say that she was feeling encouraged and that our time together was just what she needed.

I'm grateful to Alice, because this evening helped me add the option of just being present without advising or coaching to my repertoire. It's helped me to become a better professional coach, facilitator, mentor, friend, and husband.

Now when clients or friends come to me with an issue or problem, I offer them this choice: "Would you like me to just be present and listen, or shall I ask you facilitative questions to help you figure it out for yourself, or do you want me to tell you what to do?"

People love being presented with these options. Even when they opt for advice, I usually listen carefully first and ask them some questions to help clarify the challenge.

And it's also wonderful to know that you can ask someone to listen to you and just be present when you need it.

ESP: Empathy's Special Paradoxes

Light is made of waves. Light is made of particles. Physicists can explain how each of these seemingly contradictory statements is true. When apparent opposites are both true, we have a paradox. The following paradoxes shed light on how you can be more effective in building relationships.

Acceptance Makes Change Possible

> The curious paradox is that when I accept myself
> just as I am, then I can change.
> — CARL ROGERS

If you want to change something about yourself or if you want someone else to change, your efforts will probably be fruitless unless you begin with empathy and acceptance. The pioneer of client-centered therapy, Carl Rogers, called this "unconditional positive regard." As Keith McFarland experienced through his work with Al, genuine caring has a profoundly positive therapeutic effect. When clients feel accepted, they are better able to bring awareness to and begin to change behaviors that they may have deemed unacceptable.

This wisdom isn't just for therapists. It's equally relevant for leaders in every area of life: spouses, parents, managers, and colleagues.

If You Want It, Give It

> The more we hear them, the more they'll hear us.
> — MARSHALL ROSENBERG

The best way to receive more empathy is to offer it. If you want others to be more open to you, be more open to them. If you want others to listen to you, start by listening to them. In other words, be *otherish*! By listening first, you'll be offering a powerful gift of caring energy, and Givers and Matchers will naturally want to reciprocate. Even Takers may sometimes respond, but in any case you will be more informed and attuned if you make it a practice to listen first.

Most of What's Important Is Rarely Expressed Directly

I'm against picketing, but I don't know how to show it.
— MITCH HEDBERG (1968–2005), comedian

Communication would be much easier if people always said what they really mean. Of course, frequently they don't communicate directly. Sometimes it's because they don't know what they're trying to say, and other times they do know, but they're obfuscating for one reason or another. In either case, the critical skill for leaders is figuring out what other people are communicating, even when they don't express it directly.

Words and logic are important, but there's much more going on when people attempt to communicate. We must listen for emotional undercurrents that manifest in body language, voice tonality, and facial expression. We listen with our eyes as well as our ears.

Paul Ekman, author of *Emotions Revealed: Recognizing Faces and Feelings to Improve Communication and Emotional Life*, and others have attempted to catalog and analyze the varieties of facial expressions and body language that might help us figure out what someone else is actually feeling, but there's something else at play that goes deeper than the attempt to categorize external manifestations.

Aviator and poet Antoine de Saint-Exupéry (1900–1944) writes, "It is with the heart that one sees rightly; what is essential is invisible to the eye." How can we cultivate the ability to see with the heart?

Real Listening Is RARE

Think of the people you'll interact with in the week to come and consider the effect your presence will have on them. Perhaps you'll be relating to your partner or spouse, children, parents, relatives, neighbors, or friends. Maybe you'll deal with a few vendors, clerks, or taxi drivers. In the workplace you may be connecting with clients, colleagues, supervisors, or other stakeholders. How often will you be fully present in these everyday interactions? How often will others be fully present with you?

In a meta-analysis of different systems of psychotherapy, researchers found that, whatever the psychotherapeutic style, one-third of the patients seemed to improve, one-third stayed the same, and one-third got worse. Of those who improved, the patients experienced one key ingredient in common: *accurate empathy.* Sadly, the only time many of us have the experience of accurate empathy is when we pay for it in therapy. Even then, we have only a one-in-three chance of finding it.

Most people experience only very rare moments of being understood by another. Frequently, this fleeting experience becomes the basis for falling in love. In a world where people see stereotypes and can't slow down to recognize the soul of another being, the simple act of empathic listening can have a profoundly positive effect.

Here's an acronym to help you remember and practice the essentials: RARE.

R   Receive
A   Appreciate
R   Reflect
E   Enquire

Receive

Shift into a receptive mode. Let go of your preconceptions. Suspend your agenda. Be fully present. Embrace silence. Quiet your mind and open your heart, so that you can hear the feelings and needs behind the speaker's words.

Appreciate

Appreciation involves recognizing the value in people or things, and it connotes a subtle perception of aesthetic qualities. As you listen, call upon your delicate perceptions of the uniqueness and significance of the person who's speaking. Open yourself to an awareness of the beauty of his or her soul.

Reflect

Reflect back the essence of what was shared. Wherever appropriate, use the *same* key words that the speaker used, and aim to mirror the feelings and needs behind the words.

Enquire

After you reflect back the essence of what you've heard, ask the other person: "Have I understood what you said?" "Is there anything else?" Sometimes, people hesitate to ask follow-up questions, because they may be embarrassed by the tacit admission that they haven't understood what was shared. "You might fear it will make you look incompetent," explains Heidi Grant Halvorson, author of *No One Understands You and What to Do about It*, "but that's not true. Research has found that people who are inquisitive are generally judged to be more intelligent and engaged."

Of course, in our busy lives it isn't always practical to listen in this deep way. The important thing is that when it is possible and when it is crucial, you are able to do so. And for that to be the case, you'll need to solve the empath's anagram.

The Empath's Anagram

Rearrange the letters in this word:

L-i-s-t-e-n

to reveal the secret:

S-i-l-e-n-t

My mind is wildly active. I must be vigilant in the quest to re-arrange my habitual proclivities. If I didn't monitor myself, I'd be finishing other people's sentences and devoting inordinate energy to preparing my response the entire time that someone else is speaking. I've also learned that silence isn't just the key to listening to others; it is the secret of attuning to my own inner wisdom.

Cultivating the ability to be silent is the cornerstone of the art of connection, with oneself and with others. Stillness awakens our ability to tune in to our own feelings and needs and to the feelings and needs of others.

In addition to a daily meditation practice, you can also strengthen this capacity by observing periods of intentional silence. A few minutes, an hour, a half a day, or maybe even a whole day of consciously refraining from speaking (or texting, emailing, Snapchatting, etc.) generates a wonderful sense of spaciousness and quietude.

Investing in silence raises consciousness and deepens the capacity for empathy, and in very practical terms it makes it easier to avoid saying something stupid. When I was in my mid-twenties, clients began to engage me as a professional speaker and seminar leader. I'd often find myself in conversation with senior executives, renowned authors, university professors, and many other accomplished individuals. It dawned on me that I could be perceived as either a thoughtful leader or a fool, and the difference was mostly a function of what I did not say.

WAIT, WHY AM I TALKING?

Remember not only to say the right thing in the right place
but, far more difficult still, to leave unsaid
the wrong thing at the tempting moment.
— BENJAMIN FRANKLIN (1706–90),
American statesman, scientist, and philosopher

Never miss a good chance to shut up.
— WILL ROGERS (1879–1935), humorist and social critic

Let a fool hold his tongue, and he will pass for a sage.
— PUBLILIUS SYRUS

But far more numerous was the herd of such
Who think too little and who talk too much.
— JOHN DRYDEN (1631–1700), British Poet Laureate

TRIP

Another acronym to help you assess the framework for the type of listening you choose to apply is TRIP.

T   Timing
R   Relationship
I   Intention
P   Place

Timing

When you're distressed or preoccupied, deep listening may be impossible. Sometimes it's best to say, "I can't talk to you now." Trying to listen when you really can't does not work. People sense when you are not truly with them. Follow through by setting a time when you can bring your full attention to the other person. Ultimately, as Duke's Coach K. expresses it, "Leaders show respect for people by giving them time."

Relationship

Your decision whether to listen carefully and compassionately and for how long will probably be different when your colleague, child, or spouse says, "I need to talk to you," than when a telemarketer tries to sell you something. In other words, apply the power of a positive no to set the boundaries you need, so you can say yes to the relationships you choose to prioritize.

Intention

Approach every opportunity to listen with a conscious intention to be present and empathic. Without a conscious decision, we tend to react to others, judging or following preconceived notions. Instead of getting to know people, we often project stereotypes we already hold.

Place

Deep listening and real conversation are much easier if you can find a place that is free from distraction. I'm collaborating on a future book project with a good friend. He travels frequently, as I do, so it's not easy to arrange to speak to him. We recently set a time for a call, but he was delayed getting home from the airport and was attempting to speak with me from his car. I requested that we reschedule for a time when he could bring his full attention to this important conversation. He agreed. We had a wonderful inspiring conversation later in the day when he was settled at home. He wrote me a follow-up note thanking me for insisting that we speak when we were both in a place that allowed the exchange of full presence.

Empathy: Real or Faux?

My friends tell me I have an intimacy problem.
But they don't really know me.
— GARRY SHANDLING (1949–2016), comedian

Accurate empathy demands our full presence and attention. This requires clear intention. If we aren't clear, it's easy to be sidetracked into all kinds of substitutes for the real thing. Sometimes it's appropriate to give advice or offer sympathy, but these aren't the same as empathy. Well-meaning people often rely on the following responses rather than genuine empathy:

ABSOLVING: "Don't worry, you tried your best. You're not to blame."

ADVISING/INSTRUCTING: "Let me tell you how you should've handled it."

COMMISERATING: "Oh yeah, the same thing happens to me all the time."

COMPETITIVE COMMISERATING: "You think that's bad? I've got a story that is much worse."

COUNSELING BY CLICHÉ: "Everything happens for a reason. This could turn out to be a very positive lesson for you."

INVESTIGATING: "Why do you think that happened?"

OVERAFFIRMING: "Yeah, yeah. Uh-huh, uh-huh, uh-huh. Yeah." (Usually accompanied by eye contact and exaggerated head nodding.)

SPINNING: "Look at it this way, at least you got something out of it."

STEREOTYPING: "That's a typical male (female, marketing, finance, liberal, conservative, etc.) perspective."

SYMPATHIZING: "Oh, I feel so bad for you. Bummer. Bless your heart."

Real empathy emerges from the inside. An inner attitude of openness and receptivity is usually reflected in appropriate body language, eye contact, and voice tonality. Sometimes we communicate more with our presence in silence than we do by anything we say.

But words are also important. In this exercise, based on the work of Marshall Rosenberg, we will focus on the verbal expression of empathy. The following is a list of ten comments made by Pat to various colleagues, friends, and family members in the course of a week. Please consider whether the responses Pat received are accurately or faux empathic.

1. PAT: I'm confused about the meaning of empathy.

   DYLAN: Let me explain it to you again.

2. PAT: During the last week I had quite a few "bad listening" experiences. I'm getting sick of people texting while I'm speaking to them. And then my boss actually walked out of a meeting in the middle of my presentation, a presentation that he requested. It's incredibly frustrating.

   COREY: Maybe you should get them to go to a listening course?

3. PAT: I'm hopeless when it comes to separating observations from evaluations.

   ALEX: Yeah, I have trouble with that too.

4. PAT: I want to connect more deeply with the people in my life but everyone, including me, is always so busy. It's crazy! I guess I just have to make it more of a priority.

   KENDALL: So you're feeling a desire for more connection,

and you've realized you'll have to go out of your way to make it happen?

5. PAT: You're not going to believe this! Bill's secretary just called me to postpone our meeting again. I can't believe this keeps happening. It's unbelievably inconsiderate!

   AVERY: It is what it is.

6. PAT: I'm feeling really anxious, because I have to give a big sales presentation to a really difficult client on Tuesday.

   RILEY: What makes you think that client's going to be difficult?

7. PAT: Unbelievable! I was driving over here, and this huge truck cuts right in front of me. Bam! No signal, no nothing. I could've been killed.

   ROBIN: That's nothing! I actually got rear-ended yesterday, and then the driver just pulled around me and sped off.

8. PAT: I'm disappointed that my article was rejected. The editor didn't even give me a reason why!

   JESSY: Everything happens for a reason.

9. PAT: We all took the Myers-Briggs Type Indicator at work. It's fascinating, but I find it annoying that my boss keeps referring to me as a typical ENFJ.

   SHANNON: So you think there's value in the MBTI, but you feel that your boss might be misusing it?

10. PAT: I'm concerned that my memory isn't as sharp as it used to be. I forgot the time of our meeting, and I left my jacket at the coffee shop.

    TERRY: Well, just think of all the things that you didn't forget!

Here are my thoughts on the Real or Faux Empathy exercise. Do you agree or disagree?

1. PAT: I'm confused about the meaning of empathy.

   DYLAN: Let me explain it to you again.

   Faux empathy. Dylan is instructing.

2. PAT: During the last week I had quite a few "bad listening" experiences. I'm getting sick of people texting while I'm speaking to them. And then my boss actually walked out of a meeting in the middle of my presentation, a presentation that he requested. It's incredibly frustrating.

   COREY: Maybe you should get them to go to a listening course?

   Faux empathy. Corey is advising.

3. PAT: I'm hopeless when it comes to separating observations from evaluations.

   ALEX: Yeah, I have trouble with that too.

   Faux empathy. Alex is commiserating.

4. PAT: I want to connect more deeply with the people in my life but everyone, including me, is always so busy. It's crazy! I guess I just have to make it more of a priority.

   KENDALL: So you're feeling a desire for more connection, and you've realized you'll have to go out of your way to make it happen?

   Accurate empathy.

5. PAT: You're not going to believe this! Bill's secretary just called me to postpone our meeting again. I can't believe this keeps happening. It's unbelievably inconsiderate!

   AVERY: It is what it is.

   Faux empathy. Avery is counseling by cliché.

6. PAT: I'm feeling really anxious, because I have to give a big sales presentation to a really difficult client on Tuesday.

   RILEY: What makes you think that client's going to be difficult?

   Faux empathy. Riley is investigating.

7. PAT: Unbelievable! I was driving over here, and this huge truck cuts right in front of me. Bam! No signal, no nothing. I could've been killed.

ROBIN: That's nothing! I actually got rear-ended yesterday, and then the driver just pulled around me and sped off.
Faux empathy. Robin is competitively commiserating.

8. PAT: I'm disappointed that my article was rejected. The editor didn't even give me a reason why!
JESSY: Everything happens for a reason.
Faux empathy. Jessy is counseling by cliché.

9. PAT: We all took the Myers-Briggs Type Indicator at work. It's fascinating, but I find it annoying that my boss keeps referring to me as a typical ENFJ.
SHANNON: So you think there's value in the MBTI, but you feel that your boss might be misusing it?
Accurate empathy.

10. PAT: I'm concerned that my memory isn't as sharp as it used to be. I forgot the time of our meeting, and I left my jacket at the coffee shop.
TERRY: Well, just think of all the things that you didn't forget!
Faux empathy. Terry is spinning.

The Art of Interruption

I don't mean to interrupt.
I just remember random things and get excited.
— PAULA POUNDSTONE, comedian

Author Thomas Friedman proclaimed our era the "Age of Interruption." Most interruptions are obnoxious. Yesterday I was attempting to watch a football game on television. In addition to the frequent and annoying commercial breaks, the screen also featured a distracting band across the bottom with announcements of other programming.

While researching this book, I looked at a number of newspaper and magazine websites. My reading was interrupted by pop-ups aiming to recruit me into various surveys and sell me a number of things in which I haven't the slightest interest.

Constant interruptions make it difficult for us to be fully present. Paradoxically, they also distort people's sense of when it is appropriate to interrupt.

Empathic presence is the heart of great listening. It is rare and requires commitment and practice. When you are fully present and receptive, you'll be more attuned to the right moment to interrupt. Although interrupting inappropriately is a major symptom of bad listening, doing so at the appropriate time in a gracious way is an important skill to cultivate. Interrupting is the *yang* that balances the *yin* of pure receptivity.

Interruption may be appropriate when a speaker is going on too long, monopolizing a conversation to the exclusion of others, beginning to gossip, or raising inappropriate topics. Frequently people speak without really knowing what they are attempting to communicate. Interrupting with questions that facilitate greater clarity is an essential listening skill — ask any therapist or coach!

If you are a quieter and more introverted person, then you probably need to put the emphasis on the *yang* side — to be more assertive by interrupting more — whereas more extroverted, talkative folks must emphasize patience and receptivity. All of us need to recognize the importance of the balance between these two modalities. The key to the art of interrupting is to be sensitive, curious, and open to discovering appropriate timing and graceful methodology.

BE A TRAMPOLINE, NOT JUST A SPONGE

What are the characteristics that separate the very best listeners from those who are just good? In a study of 3,492 managers who were learning to be more effective coaches, Jack Zenger and Joseph Folkman discovered that the top 5 percent, as ranked by colleagues, were distinguished by the following:

They promoted discovery and insight by interrupting appropriately and respectfully to ask probing, challenging questions, questions that "gently challenge old assumptions... in a constructive way."

They were perceived as supportive and appreciative. People experienced them as expressing a genuine desire to help.

They offered helpful feedback and made useful suggestions. This surprised Zenger and Folkman, as their research showed that a common complaint about bad listeners is that they jump in to offer unwanted advice. Their data suggests, however, that *if you create a positive sense of connection* and offer advice skillfully, you will be perceived as a great listener.

The ability to be silent, present, and receptive is necessary to develop the art of listening, but it's not sufficient to master it. Masterful listeners do more than just absorb information and energy in a spongelike manner. Rather, as Zenger and Folkman conclude: "They are someone you can bounce ideas off of....They amplify, energize, and clarify your thinking. They make you feel better not merely by passively absorbing, but by actively supporting. This lets you gain energy and height, just like someone jumping on a trampoline."

The Art of Empathic Guessing

Here are brief excerpts from two of my recent conversations with clients:

MJG: Are you worried because last year's presenter offered generic, cookie-cutter ideas that didn't connect with

your smart and somewhat cynical audience? And you
want to be sure that doesn't happen again?

FIRST CLIENT (marketing assistant charged with engaging a
conference keynote): Yes, that's right.

MJG: So you need a program that will engage and inspire
your people to think more creatively, even though they
are constrained by lots of regulations?

FIRST CLIENT: Yes! Yes! That's exactly what we need!

MJG: Are you feeling frustrated because you haven't received the recognition you feel you deserve from your
boss?

SECOND CLIENT (executive vice president of a large media
company): Yeah.

MJG: And is that frustration what's keeping you up at night,
or is there something else?

SECOND CLIENT: Yes, that, but you're right. There is something else. I'm also worrying about the upcoming merger.

It wasn't too hard to make these guesses. My first client told
me that last year's presentation didn't go over well, that the feedback said that it was perceived as "cookie-cutter" and "generic," and
that she was "worried." She told me that they needed a speaker who
could "engage" and "inspire" the "very smart" but somewhat "cynical" audience. Based on what I know about her industry, I guessed
the part about being "constrained by lots of regulations."

The exchange with the second client occurred during an executive coaching session, and I reflected back in question form what I
heard the client say and what I read from observing the tension in
his face and voice. In these simple examples my clients and I connected because I mirrored back to them what they were feeling and
wanting.

But let's say my mirroring wasn't exactly accurate. The first client might have said, "I'm not really worried, just very focused." My second client might have responded, "No, I'm not frustrated. I'm furious!"

Whether the guess is right or not, what usually results, if the guess is made with a combination of caring intention and careful, centered observation, is a deepening of the connection. I love getting it right the first time, but when I don't, I learn more about those I am speaking to, and they learn that I'm *genuinely* interested in what they are actually feeling and needing now.

Psychologist William Ickes is the author of *Everyday Mind Reading: Understanding What Other People Think and Feel*. Ickes coined the term "empathic accuracy," and in his book he describes the experimental method he developed to measure this important skill. Ickes and others have discovered that skill in understanding others accurately requires a balance between emotional openness and cognitive focus. In other words, the best listeners open their hearts while sharpening their minds.

It's the same with wine. At a recent blind tasting my host was amazed when I guessed the producer, vineyard, and vintage of a delicious Pinot Noir from Oregon. My guess was predicated on some vivid sensory data. I've tasted quite a few wines from this region, and it turns out that this was one I'd enjoyed before. This pure sense memory was complemented by some careful reasoning and awareness of context — I know that the host is partial to Oregon Pinot Noir. I know that he is generous and likes to serve highly rated special wines that are more Burgundian in style.

It's fun to be right! But the real value is in bringing more attention and thoughtfulness to the wine. The same thing is true with people, except that generally they are much easier to read than Pinot Noir.

You can develop your skill in empathic guessing by becoming

more curious about what people you interact with may be feeling, needing, and wanting. Then ask them, and listen carefully to the response.

CLINICAL EMPATHY

When I contemplated going to medical school years ago, I was discouraged by the fundamental I-It assumption underlying the profession. In other words, doctors were trained to treat people as machines. In those days, admission to medical school was based on analytical abilities as measured through SAT and Medical College Admission Test (MCAT) scores and grades. Psychological understanding and relationship-building skills weren't part of the equation. Now things are beginning to change. In 2015, the American Association of Medical Colleges added questions to the MCAT designed to assess emotional intelligence. This is a reflection of a growing awareness, based on research and driven by economics, that the human element in the doctor-patient relationship plays an important role in clinical outcomes.

Prestigious institutions such as the Duke University Medical Center, Massachusetts General Hospital, and the Jefferson Medical College in Philadelphia, among many others, have begun offering empathy training to doctors. The research-validated benefits of teaching physicians to relate to patients in an I-Thou manner include:

- better clinical outcomes
- greater patient satisfaction
- reduction of treatment errors and thus a lower risk of malpractice suits
- decreased physician burnout

When it comes to a "difficult conversation," there's probably nothing more challenging than telling a patient and that patient's family to expect imminent death from cancer or another ailment. Yet most physicians still haven't been trained in communication skills or in how to manage their own emotions. The result? Depression and suicide rates that are more than double those of the general population.

Jodie Katz, medical director of the Valley Hospital Center for Integrative Medicine, observes: "In medical school we were told to leave our emotions outside the exam-room door in order to help us keep our clinical judgment clear and to protect us from feeling overwhelmed by the suffering we are attempting to mitigate. A side effect of this suppression is that we start to feel nothing at all, even positive emotions. It's an insidious process that often leads to burnout and depression."

After experiencing this for herself, Katz began an intensive study of mindfulness and the art of connecting with her patients. She learned to center herself in between appointments, so she could be fully present and empathic with each patient. Katz learned that the key to connecting with others was to connect with herself. She says, "I cultivated my ability to be present with my own natural responsiveness, including joy, pain, and sadness in the midst of a clinical encounter with a patient in a way that actually enhanced my clarity and put me into real relationship with patients who are in my care."

One result is that Katz's appointment calendar is booked consistently at least six weeks in advance by patients who appreciate her combination of empathy and expertise. Katz explains that empathy makes a physician's work much more effective and fulfilling. She reflects, "When I talk to my colleagues about the highlight of their careers, they rarely speak of making an amazing diagnosis or performing a difficult surgery; rather, they talk about an experience of connecting with a patient in a way that made a difference."

When asked to provide an example from her own practice, Katz shared the story of a patient who was in remission from glioblastoma

multiforme (a form of brain cancer) but also struggled with a debilitating eating disorder. When the tumor returned with a vengeance,
Katz was part of the team supporting her through chemotherapy and
radiation, but eventually these treatments failed. Katz recounts:

> I did everything in my power to help this patient, but all
> options were exhausted and so was she. She was in pain
> and declining rapidly, but she didn't want to go back to the
> hospital.
>
> The last time I saw her, we had one of our very difficult
> conversations. Although there was nothing I could do for
> her medically, she knew I was with her and that I would
> walk the journey with her to the end. On the way out of
> my office, she stopped and, with her now very frail hands,
> reached over to take my stethoscope off (she was so ema-
> ciated that it would have hurt her). Then she hugged me. It
> was the first time I ever received a hug from a patient.

Katz adds: "In medical school we were trained that death is a
failure. She healed a part of me with that hug. I learned that just really
being with someone in need was a gift, a gift that goes both ways."

The Empathy Spectrum

The first action movie I ever saw was a James Bond thriller with the
dapper Sean Connery in the starring role. It was only after I began
to study psychology that I realized that Bond was a psychopath. He
used his "license to kill" liberally, and rather than demonstrating re-
morse at the decapitation of a rival, he invariably had a quip to offer
instead, as satirized magnificently by Mike Myers in the *Austin Powers*
movies. Bond was also egregiously promiscuous, utilizing women
purely as objects for his short-term pleasure. Nevertheless, he was

a "good guy," and we were glad he was foiling various schemes to dominate the world.

Bond is a fictional character, but Andy McNab is real. A former member of the British Special Forces, he's a highly decorated veteran of the Gulf War who has gone on to a successful career as an author, screenwriter, and entrepreneur. McNab states, "I do know one reason why I'm successful — the main reason, in fact. It's because I'm a psychopath." He adds quickly, "But don't panic. I'm a good psychopath!"

In collaboration with psychologist Kevin Dutton, McNab wrote *The Good Psychopath's Guide to Success*. Good psychopaths, according to the authors, are able to access qualities that are essential to success in many situations, like coolness under pressure, charm, courage, and complete self-confidence. A good psychopath is able to modulate these characteristics and balance them with appropriate ethical considerations and empathy, whereas a bad psychopath uses these to ruthlessly and amorally pursue self-aggrandizement and world domination.

Simon Baron-Cohen, of the University of Cambridge, is a world authority on psychopathology and autism and the author of *Zero Degrees of Empathy: A New Theory of Human Cruelty*. He posits the notion of an empathy spectrum. He explains: "The key idea is that we all lie somewhere on an empathy spectrum. People said to be 'evil' or cruel are simply at one extreme of the empathy spectrum." At the other end of the spectrum we find individuals who are hyperempathic. Some of these folks have trouble functioning, because they feel everyone else's pain in a way that paralyzes their ability to act in service of their own needs. A bad psychopath has no concern or feelings for others and, at the other extreme, a bad empath is overly focused on others, to an unhealthy degree.

In *Against Empathy*, Yale psychology professor Paul Bloom argues that overreliance on feelings of empathy can lead us astray and generate false moral-compass readings. He maintains that empathy can lead to behavior that is prejudiced and unproductive. Hyperempathy, unmitigated by reason, may result in what Barbara Oakley, a professor of engineering at Oakland University, terms "pathological altruism." She explains: "Altruistic intentions must be run through the sieve of rational analysis; all too often, the best long-term action to help others, at both personal and public scales, is not immediately or intuitively obvious.... Indeed, truly altruistic actions may sometimes appear cruel or harmful, the equivalent of saying no to the student who demands a higher grade or to the addict who needs another hit." She makes the case that the proverbial road to hell is, indeed, often paved with good intentions, adding that misplaced "helpful" behavior frequently does more harm than good.

The challenge for aspiring leaders is to find the balance between our ability to empathize accurately and to think constructively, while acting in alignment with a higher sense of purpose and values. In practice, those who tend toward hyperempathy are well advised to "Do the opposite" and cultivate some healthy skills from the other side of the spectrum, and obviously those who are more like 007 must cultivate the ability to bond, genuinely.

When it comes to business, however, there's way too much psychopathy and, as Belinda Parmar, founder of The Empathy Business, points out, an empathy deficit. Inspired by metrics pioneered by Simon Baron-Cohen, she and her colleagues have developed a scale for rating the level of empathy that companies offer to their employees, customers, and the public. Their research demonstrates that a higher "empathy quotient" makes a company a much more enjoyable place to work, while enhancing profitability.

Despite the growing evidence for the benefits of a more empathic culture, Parmar observes that many organizations suffer from the misconception that empathy can't be measured or developed and that it is "too soft, wishy-washy, and touchy-feely." She notes:

"Empathy…is a hard skill that should be required from the board-room to the shop floor.…It can be measured, and your business's empathy quotient can be assessed, allowing CEOs to pinpoint their companies' strengths and weaknesses, and see how they rank along-side their competitors." Most important, she concludes: "The good news is that the empathy deficit can be reduced. Empathy can be learned, and companies can improve."

And what's the best way to learn empathy, reduce the deficit, and strengthen an organization's empathy quotient? Begin by culti-vating and modeling the RARE skills of listening.

The Greatest Point of Leverage

**RAISE YOUR EMPATHY QUOTIENT
BY PRACTICING LOVING-KINDNESS MEDITATION.**

Most nights before I sleep (because I know that emotions are con-tagious and I want to be a luminous glowworm), I watch videos of saints, geniuses, and positive leaders (and also comedy, especially *Seinfeld* bloopers). The other night I watched a film about the In-dian sage Neem Karoli Baba (ca. 1900–1973). It featured an inter-view with Baba Ram Dass (Richard Alpert), a prominent Harvard psychologist, and with Timothy Leary, a pioneer in psychedelic re-search. Alpert experienced enlightenment and a name change, be-coming Baba Ram Dass ("Servant of God"), when he met Neem Karoli Baba in 1967. Baba Ram Dass has lived up to the name be-stowed upon him. His charitable initiatives benefit prisoners, the dying, the hungry, the homeless, and the blind around the world. Beginning with his seminal work *Be Here Now* (1971), he's served as an inspirational teacher and a cultural icon for the transformation of consciousness.

Ram Dass explains that when he met the guru, it was the first time in his life that he felt that someone actually saw him, listened to him, and loved him for who he was, not for his achievements. The essence of his enlightenment was the realization of the power of pure empathy.

Like Carl Rogers, Ram Dass emphasizes that unconditional positive regard isn't a methodology to manipulate or change someone else. He explains: "You're looking at another being, just the way they are, and saying, 'Let me appreciate God's perfection.' You lost the key? Great. You forgot to pick up the laundry? Right." He adds: "Every time we're in the presence of unconditional love, we remember. And when we remember, we open. And when we open, the light pours through us. If you became a person who could love unconditionally, everyone you love would flower before your very eyes."

But maybe you're wondering: What does this have to do with leadership? Everything! Without wearing white robes or garlands of flowers, the finest leaders do convey a sense of unconditional positive regard. So do the happiest spouses, friends, and parents. The most important leadership skill in all walks of life is the ability to be fully present with another person, to listen with "your whole being."

According to Ram Dass: "Your sensing mechanism in life is not just your eyes, and it's not just your ears, and it's not just your analytic mind, and it's not just your skin sensitivity. It's something deeper in you. It's some quality of intuitive appreciation,...a way in which you become a receiver with all of your being, for the nature of the being of another person." He emphasizes that this is something we can all cultivate, but cautions, "You've got to understand that your ability to see the soul and subtlety inside of another person is in part dependent on your ability to acknowledge it in yourself."

Ram Dass suggests the following informal exercise to develop this capacity. Find a place where you can observe others unobtrusively and just watch people come and go. Open your heart and embrace each person you see with compassion.

A more formal and traditional version of this exercise is Loving-Kindness Meditation (LKM). This simple, easy meditation is re-search-validated to begin improving your capacity for empathy and compassion as soon as you begin practicing it.

Emma Seppälä and her colleagues found that one brief (less than ten-minute) practice session "increased feelings of social connection and positivity toward strangers." She notes that LKM "is effective in both immediate and small doses, but that it also has long-lasting and enduring effects."

There are many different versions of this practice. The one presented here is among the easiest and simplest. It takes about three minutes. (You can do it more than once if you like.)

Loving-Kindness Meditation

Ideally, find a quiet place to sit, free from distraction.

Sit so that you are aligned along your vertical axis (that's a fancy way of saying sit up at your full stature). Place your feet flat on the floor.

Extend your exhalations to slow your breathing. Then inhale through your nose into your lower belly. Allow the lower belly, ribs, and back to expand as you inhale.

Smile subtly, close your eyes gently, and keep them closed throughout the meditation.

1. *Send loving-kindness to yourself.* Silently repeat three times: "May I be safe. May I be happy. May I be peaceful and free."

2. *Send loving-kindness to a loved one.* Envision someone you love and send loving-kindness to that person. Silently repeat three times: "May you be safe. May you be happy. May you be peaceful and free."

3. *Send loving-kindness to an acquaintance.* Envision someone you interact with, but whom you don't know well, perhaps a colleague at work or a neighbor. Send loving-kindness to that person. Silently repeat three times: "May you be safe. May you be happy. May you be peaceful and free."

4. *Send loving-kindness to all humanity.* Envision the globe. Send loving-kindness to all of humanity. Silently repeat three times: "May you be safe. May you be happy. May you be peaceful and free."

5. *Send loving-kindness to yourself.* Silently repeat three times: "May I be safe. May I be happy. May I be peaceful and free."

SIX SCIENTIFICALLY VALIDATED BENEFITS OF LKM

Loving-Kindness Meditation:

1. *Increases positive emotions.* Kenan Distinguished Professor of Psychology at the University of North Carolina–Chapel Hill, Barbara Fredrickson and her colleagues found that subjects who practiced LKM for seven weeks experienced increased positive emotions, including contentment, gratitude, hope, joy, and love. These positive emotions led to other benefits, including greater clarity around purpose and a deeper sense of overall life satisfaction.

2. *Raises empathy, compassion, and feelings of social connection.* Studies by Seppälä and many others show that LKM practice enhances empathic responsiveness and "may be the most effective practice for increasing compassion."

3. *Alleviates chronic pain, PTSD, migraines, and many other health issues.* Many symptoms of these and other maladies

are associated with negative emotion. Researchers are exploring the mechanisms through which LKM helps practitioners shift into more positive emotional states. It's likely that these shifts are associated with biochemical changes that are then manifest in symptom alleviation.

4. *Slows aging.* LKM appears to effect telomere length — a marker of aging — in positive ways. Seppälä enthuses, "Throw out the expensive anti-aging creams and get on your meditation cushion!"

5. *Increases brain volume.* The areas of your brain that modulate emotional regulation will expand as you practice.

6. *Supports self-empathy and compassion.* Throughout these chapters I've emphasized that connecting with others begins with self-connection; this practice helps. One study shows that LKM alleviates depression and reduces unhealthy self-criticism while enhancing self-compassion. After a five-year study of the effects of LKM involving hundreds of subjects, Seppälä concludes: "Loving-kindness is good for you: it makes you feel happy, less focused on yourself, more connected to others."

7

Turn Friction into Momentum

Anyone can hold the helm when the sea is calm.

— PUBLILIUS SYRUS

Frances Willard (1839–98) was a pioneering advocate for women's rights who experienced tremendous resistance to her vision of gender equality. She stated, "I would not waste my life in friction when it could be turned into momentum." How can we transform friction into momentum? That's the essential question for leaders who want to manage and resolve conflict creatively.

My first experience of conflict management on the job came during the summer after college, working as a tire changer in the automotive department of Two Guys from Harrison, a long-defunct megastore in Totowa, New Jersey. On the first day at work I arrived with a copy of J. G. Bennett's *A Spiritual Psychology* under my arm. The gruff, burly shop supervisor pointed to the book and greeted me with this memorable question: "What the f--k is that?"

On most days my shift began an hour before his, and he explained that it was part of my job to punch his time card on the clock, so that he could get an extra hour of "overtime." As he explained it, "Punch me in, or I will punch you out." My other responsibility, beside changing tires, was to guard the shop when he went into the back tire-storage room to watch porn movies on a 16 mm projector while "entertaining" a variety of big-haired women who drove up to the garage in garishly painted muscle cars.

As amusing as all that was, my most vivid memory was when we were called into a meeting by the manager of the automotive department, who then explained the most important ground rule for all employees: "Okay, youse guys, listen up. We have just one rule here — don't steal more stuff than you need for your own car!"

I managed to get through the summer in one piece! Somehow I understood intuitively that I couldn't let the supervisor push me around, yet at the same time it was clear that direct opposition to his bullying tactics probably wouldn't work well either. Perhaps because the whole situation seemed so delightfully absurd, it was easier to not take threats personally and to empathize with my supervisor's perspectives on life, love, and work.

Many of the lessons in the book I held under my arm when I first walked into the auto department turned out to be most valuable in surviving the summer and in managing and resolving conflicts in my own life as well as helping clients develop their ability to find creative solutions to conflict situations.

Humility, versatility, listening, not taking things personally, separating observation from evaluation, being otherish, learning the power of a positive no, taking responsibility for our feelings and needs, and looking for the best in others are the foundation of relationship building, *and they all become more important in the face of conflict.* Managing and resolving conflict creatively and effectively also involves continuous learning and a commitment to never tire of change.

The Nature of Conflict

Preventing, managing, and resolving conflict is a critically important aspect of building relationships. One of the greatest predictors of the success or failure of a marriage, for example, is the ability to deal intelligently and compassionately with differences and disagreements, and the same thing is true in business.

The way we think about conflicts determines how we respond to them. You will be able to respond more creatively if you embrace these three attitudes:

Conflict is a normal and natural aspect of life.
Conflict is essential to the creative process.
Conflict isn't a contest.

Conflict Is a Normal and Natural Aspect of Life

> It's just a job. Grass grows, birds fly,
> waves pound the sand. I beat people up.
> — MUHAMMAD ALI (1942–2016),
> former World Heavyweight Boxing Champion

Conflict is an inescapable part of life. Thomas Jefferson observed, "An association of men who will not quarrel with one another is a thing which never yet existed, from the greatest confederacy of nations down to a town meeting or a vestry."

Skills in managing and resolving conflict are important for everyone, yet they are rarely taught in school or elsewhere. Conflict generates energy. When the energy is mishandled, it can lead to disaster. When it's dealt with intelligently, it can deepen our relationships and enrich our lives.

In H. G. Wells's classic book *The Time Machine*, we meet the Eloi, a decadent race of attractive beings who live in denial of conflict until they are eaten by the ravenous, subterranean Morlocks. At one extreme are people who deny conflict, do everything they can to avoid it, or pretend it isn't happening, and at the other extreme are those who seek it out and magnify it.

When we accept that conflict is a natural part of life and develop our ability to assess conflict situations accurately, we can begin to respond in more creative and productive ways. Conflicts are much easier to manage and resolve when we see them as creative challenges.

Conflict Is Essential to the Creative Process

> Conflict is the gadfly of thought. It stirs us to observation
> and memory. It instigates to invention. It shocks us out
> of sheeplike passivity, and sets us at noting and contriving.
> — JOHN DEWEY (1859–1952), philosopher and psychologist

Conflict is the "oxygen" of creativity, according to Sy Landau, lead author of *From Conflict to Creativity: How Resolving Workplace Disagreements Can Inspire Innovation and Productivity.* How do we utilize that oxygen to breathe life into our relationships instead of fueling explosions of wrath? The key is to think about conflict as an opportunity to generate new ideas, original solutions, and creative possibilities.

Intelligent disagreement and fruitful debate are great catalysts for the creative process. In the most creative relationships, people are able to dispense with superficial niceties and eschew political correctness. They share arguments in a forthright fashion, without impugning the character of those with whom they disagree. They don't take disagreement personally.

Harvard professor Linda Hill and her associates devoted more

than ten years to their investigation of the distinguishing characteristics of highly innovative organizations, including Pixar, Google,
eBay, and IBM. In their book entitled *Collective Genius: The Art and
Practice of Leading Innovation*, they conclude that these companies
promote diversity, collaboration, and "creative abrasion." As Hill
explained in *Scientific American*: "Creative abrasion is about having
heated, yet healthy, arguments to generate a portfolio of alternatives. People in innovative organizations have learned how to in-
quire, actively listen, and advocate for their point of view. They
understand that you rarely get innovation without diversity of
thought and conflict." Companies like those mentioned are contemporary versions of the original "innovation laboratory" developed
by inventor Thomas Edison (1847–1931), where, as Hill cites, these
notions originated.

Managers who aren't comfortable with conflict often recruit, hire,
and reward people who share their background, training, and even
their same personality type. This leads to what Dorothy Leonard
and Susaan Straus refer to as *the comfortable clone syndrome*. In a 1997
article they explain: "Because all ideas pass through similar cognitive screens, only familiar ones survive. For example, a new-business
development group formed entirely of employees with the same dis-
ciplinary background and set of experiences will assess every idea
with an unvarying set of assumptions and analytical tools. Such a
group will struggle to innovate, often in vain."

If you understand that conflict is a natural part of life and that it
can be a catalyst for creativity, you will be empowered to turn friction into momentum.

Conflict Is Not a Contest

I love sports. I love to play and to watch. Many of my most exhil-
arating moments have come in the throes of intense competition.
My opponents in basketball, wrestling, tennis, boxing, soccer, and

football push me to run faster, jump higher, and try harder than I ever could do on my own.

As a fan, I'm captivated by incredible displays of human performance that are motivated by competition. When LeBron James leaps out of nowhere to block a crucial shot in the last moments of game seven of the NBA finals and then passes to Kyrie Irving, who lofts a perfect three-pointer to win Cleveland's first title in fifty-two years, it's hard not to stand up and cheer.

Basketball, or any other sport, wouldn't be quite as thrilling if we didn't keep score. We wouldn't pay to watch Serena Williams just hit rallies with her sister; we want to see them compete, because we know, as they do, that competition will bring out their best. Tennis and basketball are contests. The goal, whatever the system of accounting, is to score more points than your opponent.

Contests can be wonderful contexts for developing skill, inspiring teamwork, and strengthening character, but the metaphor of the contest is often disastrous when applied to conflict. If you think in terms of winning or losing in conflicts, especially with your family, friends, and colleagues, you'll discover that all your victories are Pyrrhic (a Pyrrhic victory is a victory offset by vast losses).

Instead of viewing the goal of a conflict as "winning" or "being right," experiment with looking at it as a chance to learn, grow, and find creative solutions to meet people's needs. If there's a conflict over resources in your workplace, it's an opportunity to think creatively about meeting the needs of everyone involved. If you and your spouse have a disagreement over where to go on vacation, it's an invitation to think creatively about meeting one another's needs. If you try to win in the battle for resources at work without considering the needs of your colleagues, you may be successful in the short term, but you'll probably discover new problems arising and taking more of your time and energy. If you win the battle with your spouse over where to go on vacation, you'll probably discover that your partner will see to it — consciously or unconsciously — that you don't enjoy it.

And if you attempt to win in confrontations with your children by making them do what you think they should do, then you'll discover the meaning of futility. Marshall Rosenberg says: "You can't make your kids do anything. All you can do is make them wish they had. And then they will make you wish you hadn't made them wish they had."

The objective of a contest is to win. The objective of a conflict is to generate creative solutions that meet the needs of the parties involved.

Another TRIP

The TRIP acronym also helps us assess conflict situations more artfully.

T   Timing
R   Relationship
I   Intention
P   Place

Timing

If you say the right thing at the wrong time, then it's not the right thing. If you have a challenging issue to raise with a colleague or a problem to solve with your spouse, it's important to think strategically about the best time to discuss it.

Generally, the best time to address a conflict situation is sooner rather than later. If there's a fish under your table, you want to put it on top and clean it before it starts to stink. My parents have been married for more than sixty-six years, and they get along better now than ever before. One of their secrets is that they apply the advice they got from my mom's father, Jack: "Never go to bed angry."

Dr. John Gottman, known as the "Einstein of relationships" for his pioneering research into the elements that make or break marriages, has validated what Sandy and Joan learned from Grandpop Jack. Simmering negativity between partners is like a fish under the table, and the stench undermines trust, destroys alignment, and breeds contempt.

Gottman explains: "If a couple's negative events are not fully processed,...then they are remembered and rehearsed repeatedly, turned over and over in each person's mind. Trust begins to erode....As this process progresses slowly but surely, we begin to think of our partners with a universally critical eye, with suspicion and mistrust — we begin, even unconsciously, to vilify them."

This dynamic is the same in friendships and in business. The best time to address a conflict is sooner rather than later. In other words, solve problems when they're small.

Relationship

What's your relationship with the other participants in the conflict? It seems like such an obvious consideration, yet it's regularly forgotten. Is this someone you will be working with for the foreseeable future? A colleague? A neighbor? Your child? Most conflicts happen between people who have existing relationships and common interests, whether business or personal. In the United States, the majority of murders are committed by people who are acquainted with one another, and many of those homicides are perpetrated by close friends and relatives.

On the other hand, be vigilant and aim to avoid clashes with individuals with whom you do not have a relationship. Refrain from jumping out of your car to confront another motorist who may have cut you off or trying to change the behavior of people who are intoxicated and abusive (call the cops!). In other words, "Never wrestle with pigs. You both get filthy, and the pig loves it."

Intention

Some of the greatest fighters in the history of boxing, like Mike Tyson or Jack Dempsey, were renowned for hitting their opponents with "bad intentions." A boxing match is a contest, and hitting this way helped Dempsey and Tyson become champions.

Championing a creative approach to conflict requires us to train ourselves to consciously choose our intention for the outcome and, when possible, to empathize with the needs underlying the intention of the other party. Instead of reflexively going for the knockout when conflict arises, consider these essential questions: "What might be the intention of the other party in the conflict?" "What's my intention for the outcome?"

Everything people do is in service of their needs, consciously or otherwise. When we understand the needs that are driving our own behavior and the needs underlying the behavior of others, we are better able to understand and respond creatively.

Place

Timing and place go together for better or for worse. The worst place to address a conflict with a colleague or your spouse is in "public." As Leonardo da Vinci advised five hundred years ago, "Reprove a friend in private, praise him in public."

In combat arts, your place, or position, is critical. Taking the high ground in a battle or controlling the center of the board in chess is often the key to victory. Awareness of place is also important in addressing everyday conflicts creatively.

If, for example, you'd like to facilitate a creative approach to resolving a conflict between your marketing department and your engineering group, or between your science faculty and your humanities teachers, or between you and your spouse, think carefully about where you'll meet. If you're meeting in the office, school, or home, then think about how you'll arrange the furniture. When people face one another directly across a table — as is often the case in negotiations — they tend, as Roger Fisher, cofounder of the Harvard Negotiation Project, explains, "to respond personally and engage in...argument." Fisher advises, "People sitting side by side in a semicircle of chairs facing a blackboard tend to respond to the problem depicted there." In other words, if you organize the space in accordance with the idea of "separating the people from the problem," you'll discover that it's easier for everyone to avoid taking things personally, thereby liberating more energy to invent options for mutual gain.

And, if you want to promote a creative approach, it's often best to get out of the office, school, or home altogether. Many people discover that problems that seem insoluble when they're sitting across the table become more susceptible to solutions when they're walking in nature.

So be creative about where you meet. When I asked Evan Shepard, the CEO of a global conglomerate, what he had learned after years of contending with all kinds of lawsuits, disputes, and challenging negotiations, he responded, "Don't meet in the lawyer's office!" He offered the following examples:

> We had a serious dispute with some folks we had been doing business with for years. They wanted to meet at the lawyer's office and fight it out.
>
> In happier times we had all gone skiing together. So I proposed that we meet at a ski resort in Utah. I skied down the mountain with my counterpart, and my general counsel skied with her counterpart. Then we sat around the fire to consider solutions. Then we went out for another beautiful ski run. The issues that had seemed intractable when we

raised them initially were all resolved in a couple of days, and we all had a great time.

On another occasion we were being sued by a firm based in Wisconsin. It was February, the dead of winter. We knew we had some responsibility for what had gone wrong and wanted to sort it out. Everyone in our industry told us how much the Wisconsin group loved golf. So we invited them at our expense to meet at a golf resort in Tucson. We got the dispute settled in four hours in the morning, because we had made tee times for them in the afternoon. We got the thing done for a tiny fraction of what it would've cost to litigate. Of course they knew what we were doing, but it worked anyway, because they sensed that we were making a genuine expression of goodwill and taking responsibility for what had gone wrong.

Don't Make It Worse

When you are aware of the timing, relationship, intention, and place, you are much more likely to be able to apply the first rule of conflict management: *Don't make it worse.* If you reflect on the major conflicts you've experienced in your life thus far, whether at home or at work, you'll probably be able to remember a time when you said or did something that made the situation worse.

It's okay to feel angry, but some ways of expressing it are much more constructive than others. It's fine to hit your pillow or scream in the shower (as long as you shower alone). It's okay to write an angry email, just DPS (Don't Press Send!). Dance, poetry, and art all allow us to express our feelings constructively. Run ten miles, hit the heavy bag, play racquetball, but don't act out your anger in a way that exacerbates the situation.

An ancient Chinese proverb advises, "If you are patient in one moment of anger, you will escape a hundred days of sorrow."

Avoid personal enmity. Eschew personal attacks and insults, no matter how justified you may think they are in any given situation. They always make things worse.

Prevention is easier than resolution. What's the best time to deal with people problems? It's before they become people problems! If you cultivate the ability to avoid taking things personally, then you will not need to attend every argument to which you are invited. Then, when things go wrong, you won't feel compelled to go with them.

If you don't make it worse, then it's much easier to figure out how you might make it better.

The Way of Harmonious Energy

One should be in harmony with, not in opposition to,
the strength and force of the opposition.
— BRUCE LEE (1940–73), martial arts icon

The "Way of Harmonious Energy," a.k.a. aikido, was originated in Japan by Morihei Ueshiba. Known as O-Sensei ("Great Teacher"), he was a gifted martial artist and spiritual seeker. Ueshiba was dissatisfied with the injuries and violence that were part of the highly competitive, win-lose structure of martial contests. One day a high-ranking naval officer who was renowned as an expert sword fighter challenged Ueshiba to a contest. Despite his philosophical objections, he felt compelled by the etiquette of the time to accept. According to witnesses, the challenger tried with all his might and skill to strike Ueshiba down with blows from his heavy wooden sword (known as a *bokken*). But each time the sword came down, Ueshiba managed to evade the attack. This continued until the exhausted challenger surrendered.

Afterward, Ueshiba went to his garden, where he experienced enlightenment. As he described it:

I felt the universe suddenly quake, a golden spirit sprang up from the ground, veiled my body, and changed my body into a golden one. At the same time my body became light. I was able to understand the whispering of the birds, and was clearly aware of the mind of God, the creator of the universe. At that moment I was enlightened: the source of Budo [martial arts] is God's love — the spirit of loving protection for all beings.

When I was growing up in Passaic, New Jersey, "golden light" and the "whispering of the birds" didn't inform my attitude toward conflict. I was voted "Class Arguer" in my senior year of high school, and I relished the opportunity to eviscerate opponents in debate.

This was the time of the Vietnam War and major racial conflict as well. The world seemed divided in to opposing camps and conflict was everywhere. (Actually, kind of like the situation now.) My interest in creative thinking evolved during this time, as it seemed to be the greatest point of leverage for addressing the problems of humanity. (Now I think it takes creative thinking combined with the art of connection.)

In addition to being Class Arguer, I was also on the wrestling team. In one match, I was applying a hold to my opponent known as a "tight waist" — the aim of which is to squeeze your opponent's gut as hard as possible — and he coughed up blood. Now the thing about wrestling is that you are facing someone who is your weight and age, someone a lot like you. Although I won the match, I couldn't stop thinking about this fellow, who was a lot like me, spitting blood. My ideals started to turn toward peace and love (popular notions in those days), but my aggressive energy and attraction to sports and martial arts continued unabated.

When I was twenty the television show *Kung Fu* debuted. In the pilot episode, the blind master begins to refer to his disciple as "Grasshopper" after this scene:

MASTER: Close your eyes. What do you hear?
DISCIPLE: I hear the water, I hear the birds.
MASTER: Do you hear your own heartbeat?
DISCIPLE: No.
MASTER: Do you hear the grasshopper which is at your feet?
DISCIPLE: Old man, how is it that you hear these things?
MASTER: Young man, how is it that you do not?

The disciple eventually became a master in his own right — Kwai Chang Caine, as played by David Carradine — and I was captivated by his example of grace and poise in the face of conflict.

Then, a few years later, I witnessed a diminutive aikido master tossing bigger, younger, and stronger attackers around effortlessly. The master had a bemused expression throughout the demonstration, and the attackers seemed energized and inspired by the graceful way in which their force was redirected. This seemed to be a real-life manifestation of the kung fu saga, complete with an enlightened ethical philosophy, so I began intensive training.

Over the years I've trained with many of the original students of Ueshiba. Most of these contemporary masters were resident students of the founder when they were teenagers, and quite a few of them were already skilled in other martial arts when they arrived. How did O-Sensei win over these testosterone-hyped teenage judo and karate champions who would ultimately become global ambassadors for the Way of Harmonious Energy? The main reason they all became so receptive to his ideals of loving-kindness and protection of all beings is because this four-foot-eleven older man could mop the floor with all of them!

I complemented my study of aikido with exploration of other arts that did not share the philosophical commitment to peaceful conflict resolution. I was curious about the practical application of the Way of Harmonious Energy in situations that weren't scripted, but my main focus has never been fighting. Rather, I wanted learn how to keep my poise in challenging situations and how to assess and manage aggression in different forms. Seventh-degree black belt and author of *Leadership Embodiment*, Wendy Palmer suggests: "Aikido is ultimately about learning a more enlightened way to connect with others, to have a more creative conversation when there's a disagreement or conflict."

Here's a simple formula drawn from the art of aikido that can help you have more enlightened connections and productive conversations. It's called *center and blend*.

Centering

In the 1990s I trained regularly at the dojo of Mitsugi Saotome Shihan, one of the great contemporary aikido masters. A resident student with O-Sensei for fifteen years before being sent to the United States to represent the art, Saotome shared many stories of his time with Ueshiba. He recounted the awe with which all the resident students beheld their master.

On one occasion Saotome exclaimed to his teacher: "Your techniques are perfect! You never make any mistakes. You never lose your center!"

O-Sensei replied, "I lose my center frequently. I just find it again so quickly that you can't see it."

The ability to apply any of the lessons in this book is predicated on the skill of centering. It's a skill that anyone can learn, and it is the ability that makes all other relationship and leadership skills possible.

Centering is the ability to bring your full attention and intelligence to the present moment without prejudice. It is a state characterized by a balance between alertness and relaxation, also known as *poise* or *flow*. Centering is essential to our emotional intelligence, because emotional intelligence begins with self-control.

Conflicts large and small often cause us to "lose it." The critical question is: How can you get "it" — your physical/emotional balance — back quickly and seamlessly? The key to developing centering skill is to *practice every day in nonthreatening situations*, so you can call on the skill when you're under stress.

Legendary martial artist Miyamoto Musashi advises: "In all forms of strategy, it is necessary to maintain the combat stance in everyday life and to make your everyday stance your combat stance. You must research this well." The "combat stance" to which Musashi refers is upright, balanced, relaxed, and alert. If you cultivate these qualities when you are reading a book, cooking in your kitchen, talking on the phone, or walking to your car, you will be much better at applying them when you are interrupted while giving an important presentation or conducting a complex and challenging negotiation.

When you're first learning to drive, it can be pretty scary when a huge truck is speeding toward you on the other side of a two-lane highway. After more experience in the driver's seat, you find yourself unfazed by the same phenomenon. When I began martial arts training, it was difficult to avoid reacting with tension and fear when a burly opponent threw a punch or kick at my head; now it's just part of the scenery. And most people find it easier to learn how to stay centered driving or even sparring than when someone disrespects, insults, or attempts to take advantage of them.

In neuroscientific terms centering is the process of preventing or recovering from the "amygdala hijack," a term introduced by Daniel Goleman in his book *Emotional Intelligence: Why It Can Matter More Than IQ*. Our brain's primitive alarm center for warning of danger, the amygdala is the launching pad of the fight-or-flight response. This response is a survival mechanism that mobilizes our body to flee or be ready to fight when confronted by, for example, a saber-toothed tiger. It operates much faster than our rational, verbal mind. This worked well for our Pleistocene ancestors on the plains of Africa, but it isn't as adaptive on the highway, where road rage results in accidents and lawsuits, or in the office, where fleeing from a difficult encounter with your boss or punching him in the head will probably result in long interviews with HR.

The amygdala hijack happens suddenly, before you realize it. It is characterized by intense emotions and powerful physiological changes, and it usually leads to regrets. Developing emotional intelligence is based on learning the ability to reassert the brain's executive control center to foil the hijack before you do something you will regret. This is what O-Sensei meant when he spoke of "finding his center again so quickly that nobody can see it." This is an important aspect of personal growth and a critical leadership skill.

There are many approaches to centering, and all are predicated on returning your brain to "executive control." The key is to interpose a delay between the stimulus and the response. In other words, to *pause*. Thomas Jefferson understood this when he advised: "When angry, count to ten before you speak. If very angry, a hundred."

Every martial art begins with centering. If you want to vanquish an opponent, then it's better to be centered. You'll discover more options for your own gain and more efficient means to punish your enemy, if you're poised and balanced rather than enraged and crazed.

Aikido is based on the idea that we are all connected through a fundamental universal harmony and that the task of the martial artist is to view any attack as an opportunity to restore the natural state of peace. That is why aikido does not promote competition or combat. It's much easier to learn how to hurt someone else than it is to learn how to protect yourself using minimal force and causing no unnecessary damage to the person who attacked you.

Centering makes it possible to consider this illuminating ethical choice in the face of conflict. *Blending* is the key to implementing it.

Blending

The syllable *ai* in *aikido* translates as "harmony" or "blending." Rather than confronting an oncoming attack directly, aikido training emphasizes avoiding and then skillfully redirecting the force, so that it harmlessly dissipates.

In 1980, I helped to arrange for a senior Japanese master to offer an aikido demonstration for a corporate leadership team as part of a five-day seminar on the theme "Balancing the Brain." The master invited his most advanced student, who was about six foot two and quite formidable in his own right, to attack him with a large wooden sword (*bokken*). The master asked the student to strike as fast and hard as he could and explained that it would be a grave insult for his student to attack with anything less than the intent to kill! Wielding the weapon with the aplomb of a veteran samurai, the student let out a piercing scream (known in Japanese as a *kiai*) as he leapt toward the master, aiming to strike right through the top center of his teacher's head.

A moment before his skull would have been pulverized, the master eased off the line of the attack and moved seamlessly to match his movement with the attacker's. The result was that the master was now side by side with his attacker, facing the same direction, with his hand assuming control of the attacker's hand and the sword. The master led the sword down toward the floor so that the attacker's head bobbled, and the next thing we saw was the attacker flying through the air while the weapon remained in the master's hand. Everyone in the group held their breath and then applauded wildly. The master bowed, paused, and said, "Very important when sword comes down, *get out of way!* Otherwise, two sides of brain will separate."

The ability to get out of the way and harmonize with an oncoming force is the most distinctive aspect of aikido. This harmony in action is known as blending.

"A Kind Word Turneth Away Wrath"

Terry Dobson (1937–92) was one of the first Westerners to be a resident student of the founder of aikido. His book *Aikido in Everyday Life* is a seminal work in the practical application of the Way of Harmonious Energy to building relationships and resolving conflict. I was blessed with the opportunity to attend his seminars and have him throw me around the mat.

Terry wrote a story about learning the essence of aikido that I have shared with executive groups around the world for decades. The original title is "A Kind Word Turneth Away Wrath" (inspired by the biblical proverb, "A soft answer turneth away wrath, but grievous words stir up anger").

Terry's life changed one day when he was riding a train through the suburbs of Tokyo in the spring of the fourth year he spent in residence as a disciple of Morihei Ueshiba. A former linebacker, Dobson was a formidable presence, and in those days he was training eight hours a day with the master. Terry was usually the prime subject in Ueshiba's public demonstrations, as it was especially impressive for Japanese audiences to witness the four-foot-eleven O-Sensei toss the gigantic Westerner around like a rag doll.

Although Terry was an earnest student of the philosophy of the Way of Harmonious Energy, he, like many who pursue intensive martial study, had a strong aggressive streak. He noted, "I loved to grapple and mix it up. I thought I was tough." But he confessed, "Trouble was, my martial skill was untested in actual combat."

Terry took Ueshiba's teaching to heart. Ueshiba had emphasized: "Aikido is the art of reconciliation.... Whoever has the mind to fight has broken his connection with the universe. If you try to dominate people, you are already defeated. We study how to resolve conflict, not how to start it." Terry struggled with the tension between this noble, exalting ideal and his darker, testosterone-fueled desire to prove what he could do in a real fight.

He forced himself to cross the street rather than engage with the teenage hoodlums who loitered near the entrance to his local train station. But he confessed, "In my heart, however, I wanted an absolutely legitimate opportunity whereby I might save the innocent by destroying the guilty."

The opportunity presented itself on that spring day when the quiet rhythm of the train ride was disturbed by the sudden, violent entrance of a huge, filthy, drunken Japanese laborer who started screaming vile curses as he shoved a woman holding her baby out of his way. Miraculously, she landed safely in the arms of an elderly couple sitting across the aisle.

Terry said, "The train lurched ahead, and the passengers froze with fear. I stood up." As Terry rose from his seat ready to intervene, the drunk focused his fury, cursing the foreigner whom he swore was about to receive a "lesson in Japanese manners."

This was the moment for which Terry had been waiting! A justifiable opportunity to use his skills in defense of the innocent and to punish the guilty.

Terry's street instinct took over, and he gave his adversary "a slow look of disgust and dismissal" followed by blowing him an "insolent kiss," tactics designed to cause an amygdala hijack and incite him to make the first move. Poised to "take this turkey apart," Terry watched as the drunk tightened his fists in preparation for the assault.

Then, as Terry recounted:

> A split second before he could move, someone shouted "Hey!" It was ear splitting. I remember the strangely joyous, lilting quality of it — as though you and a friend had been searching diligently for something, and he suddenly stumbled upon it. "Hey!"
>
> I wheeled to my left; the drunk spun to his right. We both stared down at a little old Japanese man. He must have

been well into his seventies, this tiny gentleman, sitting there immaculate in his kimono. He took no notice of me, but beamed delightedly at the laborer, as though he had a most important, most welcome secret to share.

"C'mere," the old man said in an easy vernacular, beckoning to the drunk. "C'mere and talk with me." He waved his hand lightly.

The big man followed, as if on a string. He planted his feet belligerently in front of the old gentleman and roared above the clacking wheels, "Why the hell should I talk to you?" The drunk now had his back to me. If his elbow moved so much as a millimeter, I'd drop him in his socks.

The old man continued to beam at the laborer. "Whatcha been drinking?" he asked, his eyes sparkling with interest.

"I been drinking sake," the laborer bellowed back, "and it's none of your business!" Flecks of spittle spattered the old man.

"Oh, that's wonderful," the old man said, "absolutely wonderful! You see, I love sake too. Every night, me and my wife — she's seventy-six, you know — we warm up a little bottle of sake and take it out into the garden, and we sit on an old wooden bench. We watch the sun go down, and we look to see how our persimmon tree is doing. My great-grandfather planted that tree, and we worry about whether it will recover from those ice storms we had last winter." He looked up at the laborer, eyes twinkling.

As he struggled to follow the old man's conversation, the drunk's face began to soften. His fists slowly unclenched. "Yeah," he said. "I love persimmons too." His voice trailed off.

"Yes," said the old man, smiling, "and I'm sure you have a wonderful wife."

"No," replied the laborer. "My wife died." Very gently, swaying with the motion of the train, the big man began to sob. "I don't got no wife, I don't got no home, I don't got no job. I am so ashamed of myself." Tears rolled down his cheeks; a spasm of despair rippled through his body.

Now it was my turn. Standing there in my well-scrubbed youthful innocence, my make-this-world-safe-for-democracy righteousness, I suddenly felt dirtier than he was.

Then the train arrived at my stop. As the doors opened, I heard the old man cluck sympathetically. "My, my," he said. "That is a difficult predicament, indeed. Sit down here and tell me about it."

I turned my head for one last look. The laborer was sprawled on the seat, his head in the old man's lap. The old man was softly stroking the filthy, matted hair.

As the train pulled away, I sat down on a bench. What I had wanted to do with muscle had been accomplished with kind words. I had just seen aikido in combat, and the essence of it was love.

The old man on the train was the true master of aikido principles.

A few years ago I experienced a similar but much less dramatic version of the same lesson that Terry learned. My wife and I were visiting the Louvre Museum, and we went to see the *Mona Lisa*. It was crowded, and people were jostling around trying to take photographs of Leonardo da Vinci's masterpiece, despite the many "No Photography" signs. I allowed myself to be annoyed by people not actually looking at the painting except through their cameras, and the irony is that my focus on the evaluation of others in this scenario wasn't contributing to my mindful appreciation of the painting. Now, that realization is humbling enough, but there's more.

As we ambled our way as close to Leonardo's masterpiece as is possible, a man turned suddenly and jutted out his device directly toward my wife's face in an attempt to take a selfie with Mona. I swatted his hand away and scolded him abruptly (I did inhibit my desire to throw him across the room).

What happened next was my mini version of Terry's lesson. A woman next to us asked the gentleman if he would like her to take his photo, and he happily agreed. I realized that I could have gently redirected the man's arm without responding so defensively and that I could've been more empathic with his need to immortalize his moment with Mona. In other words, I could have chosen not to have taken it personally and instead blended with my "attacker." Upon reflection it's clear that he was just excited about the moment and meant no harm.

Radical Blending: It's All About Making a Connection

"I've just entered the hospital treatment room at the request of the police lieutenant in charge of the hostage situation. Sam is holding a scissors to Sheila's throat and he's threatening to kill her, me, and as many other people as he can.

"My question for you is: What would you say, what would you do if you were in that situation?"

That's the question posed by George Kohlreiser, a hostage negotiator with forty years of experience, the author of two award-winning books, and a professor of leadership at IMD Switzerland. George has been held hostage himself four times. Here's George's description of what happened next:

> Sam cut Sheila on the side of her neck, but didn't slice through her jugular or windpipe. She started bleeding and screaming, and he stepped back and charged with the scissors pointed directly at me. I had a nanosecond to decide

what to do. Should I yell for the police to shoot him or throw my body at his feet, or should I try to talk to him?

I chose to try talking, even as he put the scissors to my throat and pressed the point into my skin. Instinctively, I put my hands up around his arms, and looking into his eyes, I saw intense rage and hatred at the same time that I felt his sense of deep grief and utter desperation.

I asked, "Sam, how would you like your children to remember you?"

He said, "Don't ever talk about my children. I will kill them too! I have no hope. I have nothing to live for. I am ready to die."'

George comments:

On the surface this sounds pretty negative, but it's not. Why? It's the first moment that Sam and I connected, through a negative transaction about killing his kids. And after another twenty minutes of dialogue, he allowed Sheila to leave the room, and shortly after, he then gave me the scissors (which I promptly threw on the floor). Then he allowed himself to be handcuffed and taken to a secure unit of the hospital for the treatment of a life-threatening stab wound that he had come to the hospital for in the first place.

Later he told me: "George, you're okay. I'm glad I didn't kill you."

I asked George how he was able to turn this situation around. He responded, "It's all about making a connection."

George explains that hostage negotiators are successful in about 95 percent of these types of situations. I asked him the secrets of connecting under these very stressful circumstances. He explains that the first priority is to recover your own center, to manage your own stress. He adds that it helps to remember that you don't have to like someone in order to form a bond with that person. As he states it: "Hostage negotiators create a bond with some of the most despicable people you can imagine."

It's difficult for most of us to imagine how we might maintain a sense of connection with a despicable person. How is it possible to connect with a person who has a gun to your head or a scissors against your neck?

George answers "*Empathy!*" He explains that people don't take hostages unless they are hostage themselves to deep pain, desperation, rage, and fear. They are always acting out of a sense of profound loss and inner agony.

It's one thing to feel empathy, but how do you demonstrate it under extreme conditions when your life, and perhaps the lives of others, are being threatened?

George answers: "I always speak to the hostage taker with respect for his dignity and show interest in him. I ask questions rather than making statements or demands. Questions inspire engagement and are the essence of dialogue. When the hostage taker begins to engage with me in a dialogue, then it's much less likely that he will kill me, because people don't kill people, they kill objects or things. In order to kill, dehumanization has to take place first. By asking questions and listening, I 'humanize' the interaction."

George explains that in the situation with Sam he humanized the interaction by asking about his children. As the dialogue evolved, he posed questions at every stage in order to affirm Sam's dignity. The most impactful question was, "Sam, how do you want your children to remember you? Do you want them to remember you as a murderer?"

And instead of just saying, "Sam, give me the scissors," George asked, "Sam, will you give me the scissors or do you want to throw them on the floor?" And when it came time for him to be handcuffed,

George asked him if he wanted to be handcuffed with his hands in front or behind.

George teaches these principles at an international business school. Although most of the leaders he counsels don't have to worry about being taken hostage physically, George emphasizes that the important point is not to be a hostage psychologically, either by others or by oneself.

The Principal of Blending

Pete Reilly is a teacher, author, and aikido practitioner. He shares a story about the power of blending to turn friction into momentum:

> Several years ago, I watched in awe as a veteran principal blended with a disgruntled teacher who had been challenging some of the ideas being discussed during his school's staff-development program. The teacher was clearly frustrated and eventually blurted out angrily, "I'd like permission to leave. This program is stupid, and it's not relevant. I'd rather go back to my classroom and do some lesson planning."
>
> The presenter reacted as if he'd been punched in the stomach, and the entire staff looked stunned. The principal, who was sitting in the back of the room, broke the ensuing silence and spoke in a measured and sincere manner: "We're not asking for you to adopt every idea that's being presented in the program. But why not give it till the lunch break and see if there might be a few things that you can use to help you?"
>
> The teacher protested, "I've got better things to do with my time."
>
> The principal continued to blend. "You've already brought a lot to the program by challenging some of the ideas [the presenter] has brought forth. I think you surfaced

a few thoughts that some in the group may have been thinking about, but weren't willing to verbalize. We need people like you, with different points of view, to be active and vocal, so that the learning here is real. The worst thing that could happen is we leave this session and have the real discussion and questions relegated to complaints in the teachers' room."

The principal sat quietly looking at the angry teacher, who was surprised by the principal's openness. His face began to soften, and the moment opened in possibility.

The teacher nodded his head, saying, "If you think it will help, I'll give it a try."

The principal smiled warmly. "It will. Thanks."

Pete adds, "I'd never seen a 'blend' done so well anywhere outside of an aikido dojo."

Blending to Save a Fortune

Evan, the CEO, explains how he "blended" to settle what might have been a protracted and costly lawsuit:

We were being sued by a fellow who was injured when he was working around some equipment our company made. His injury was not serious, and yet he was seeking significant damages. Usually when something like this happens, most attorneys would just assume that it's an unavoidable adversarial situation where someone is just trying to exploit our relatively deep pockets. But we encourage a culture of thinking creatively and being empathic in all our interactions, so our lead attorney explored the situation with an open mind and discovered that the fellow who was bringing the case wasn't necessarily avaricious.

She learned that he was having a rough time in his

marriage and that he felt generally unhappy in his life. She intuited that he needed to feel a greater sense of connection with himself and his wife, and she asked if he would please drop the action against us if we treated him and his wife to a long weekend at a five-star beach resort, including covering child care, so that he and his wife could reconnect.

He accepted our offer, and I was delighted, not just because it saved us a fortune, but also because my guess is that this outcome enriched his life much more than a protracted court battle would have.

The old man on the train was able to empathize with the pain and suffering of the drunken laborer, so that he could defuse a dangerous situation. George Kohlreiser was able to put himself in Sam's shoes even with scissors at his throat, and in the process he saved not only his own life, but also Sam's, as a police sniper was ready to pull the trigger if necessary. The principal was able to keep a dialogue going in what could easily have been a disastrous situation, and Evan was able to save his company a fortune while enriching the quality of life of his former adversary.

If you can recover your center fast enough so that you can choose to blend with and redirect an attacker's energy, you'll be in a much better position, figuratively and physically, to lead the situation to a creative resolution.

Blend to Invent Options for Mutual Gain

Roger Fisher (1922–2012) served as a reconnaissance pilot in World War II and then graduated from Harvard Law School, becoming a professor there in 1958. Witnessing maiming and death firsthand during the war and then seeing the destructive effects of costly, protracted litigation as a partner in a major law firm, Fisher was passionate about finding more creative alternatives to resolve conflict.

In 1979 he cofounded the Harvard Negotiation Project, where

he and his colleagues sought out the most skilled negotiators to learn and codify their strategies. Over the years they applied what they learned to help many companies and institutions resolve conflict, while also consulting with those who were aiming to bring peaceful resolutions to some of the world's most intractable political conflicts. (Fisher played a key role in advising President Carter in brokering the peace deal between Egypt and Israel.)

In 1991 he and William Ury published the classic bestseller *Getting to YES*. Fisher and those who have followed in his footsteps discovered that the most effective negotiators, whether in business or in mediating global conflict, are skilled in the art of connection. They manage their own emotions (centering), and they focus on blending (empathizing and connecting) with the other side's point of view, before offering creative solutions designed to meet the needs of all the parties involved (inventing options for mutual gain).

Fisher and Ury describe the importance of blending, of empathy, in the face of conflict: "The ability to see the situation as the other side sees it, as difficult as it may be, is one of the most important skills a negotiator can possess." They emphasize that this is more than just an intellectual process in which we understand that others may see things differently than we do. Rather, we must empathically experience the "emotional force" that animates their point of view. "It is not enough to study them like beetles under a microscope; you need to know what it feels like to be a beetle," they say.

They explain how the art of connection sets the stage for effective conflict resolution and negotiation: "The more quickly you can turn a stranger into someone you know, the easier a negotiation is likely to become.... Find ways to meet them informally.... A note of sympathy, a statement of regret, a visit to a cemetery, delivering a small present for a grandchild, shaking hands or embracing, eating together — all may be priceless opportunities to improve a hostile emotional situation at small cost."

Once we understand the feelings, needs, and interests of the other side in a conflict or negotiation, we are obviously in a much better position to discover creative solutions. Fisher and Ury advise, "Invent several options all equally acceptable to you and ask the other side which one they prefer."

The ability to invent options for mutual gain is predicated on your skill at recovering your center. When you're centered, you are able to clarify the situation (assess the TRIP: timing, relationship, intention, place) and separate the people from the problem and observations from evaluations.

Before looking for creative solutions remember: *Conjungere ad solvendum*, Connect before solving. Attune to and empathize (blend) with feelings: "How do I/they feel about the situation?" "What are the underlying needs that I/they have in this situation?"

Once you're connected and attuned to underlying feelings and needs, you'll discover that it's much easier to think creatively about solutions. Turn friction into momentum by asking: "Is there anything that I/they haven't thought of yet that might meet the needs that I/they have in this situation?"

Sweet Fruit from the Bitter Tree

The stories of Terry, George, the principal, and Evan are just a few of my favorites. You can reinforce a creative attitude toward conflict by enjoying more inspiring stories like these. Mark Andreas spent seven years compiling the stories in his book *Sweet Fruit from the Bitter Tree: 61 Stories of Creative and Compassionate Ways out of Conflict*. Mark explains that in every story he collected positive outcomes were achieved because those involved kept or recovered their connection, first with themselves and then with others.

What does Mark believe to be the core secret to successful conflict resolution?

He responds, "In a word, my answer is: connection."

The Greatest Point of Leverage

CULTIVATE THE ABILITY TO ORGANIZE YOUR NERVOUS SYSTEM.

I'm not going to stop torturing myself
till I figure out the cause of my pain.
— MATT GROENING, creator of *The Simpsons*

The New York Aikikai is one of the world's premier places to study
the Way of Harmonious Energy. The oldest continuously operating dojo in the continental United States, it is located in Chelsea,
an area of Manhattan that is now considered prime real estate, but
when the school first opened in the 1960s it wasn't the nicest neighborhood. The Aikikai considers allowing students the opportunity
to test for the rank of black belt after an average of four years of regular, devoted training. Testing for black belt is an important rite of
passage.

One of the legendary stories from the early days of the dojo
involves a young man named Phil, who after fulfilling all the prereq-
uisites was granted permission to test. He passed and was elated. On
his walk home he was so caught up in thinking about his new, ex-
alted status that he almost failed to notice that someone had crossed
the street behind him and was now following him. Fortunately, he
became aware just in time to also notice that another suspicious person was crossing the street in front of him. Aware of the potential
danger, he did what he was trained to do. He brought his full attention to the present moment, lengthened his spine, softened his
gaze, deepened his breathing, and smiled as he extended his energy
out in all directions. The would-be muggers sensed that this was
not someone they wanted to mess with, and as they fled the scene
Phil heard one of them say to the other, "I think we've got the
wrong guy!"

Now Phil was really pleased with himself! He turned around, ran back to the dojo, and told the master about his triumph. The master frowned and said, "Not so good! Had you really mastered aikido, they never would've crossed the street in the first place."

In a classic study imprisoned muggers were asked to rate the muggability of people by simply watching them walk down the street. The study concluded that the most attractive targets were people whose gait was perceived as "nonsynchronous." In other words, if you are walking down the street while texting or simply not paying attention, as was the case with Phil before he centered himself, you're more likely to be assaulted. The distinguishing aspect of those who were perceived as unappealing victims was "a 'wholeness' or consistency of movement." They possessed an "organized quality about their body movements." Fortunately, Phil knew how to organize himself quickly.

Although it's unlikely that you will be physically attacked when you walk into a conference room to give a presentation or into your living room to deal with a problem with your spouse or children, everyone in all these contexts will instantly and automatically assess your muggability.

Skill in preventing, managing, or resolving conflict with others requires a continuing process of preventing, managing, or resolving our internal conflicts. The greatest point of leverage for resolving conflict internally, and externally, is to *cultivate the ability to organize your nervous system*, and to reorganize quickly when you feel threatened or stressed.

This ability is the greatest point of leverage for everything in the whole book. When you are centered and present, you are able to connect, and when you connect, you can blend and lead.

The key is to practice centering every day when it's not urgent, so you can do it when it is. Here's an acronym to help you organize your nervous system to prevent or resolve conflict.

RESOLVE

R   Remember to pause
E   Exhale
S   Smile
O   Observe
L   Lengthen your spine
V   Visualize
E   Expand and empathize

Remember to Pause

Pause, so you can affirm your intention. Conflict is natural; it's an opportunity to be creative, and it isn't a contest. What outcome do you want? If you can pause and affirm a positive intention in what seems like a negative situation, you'll shift your physiology and psychology to a more resourceful state.

Exhale

Exhale fully. You can whisper an extended "Ahhhh" sound to release your breath. Then inhale through your nose into your lower belly. Allow the lower belly, ribs, and back to expand as you inhale. Then extend your exhalation to slow your breathing. The fight-or-flight response is characterized by rapid, shallow breathing. Slowing and deepening the breath instantly move your biochemistry toward relaxation.

Smile

Imitate the subtle smile of the *Mona Lisa*. Smiling also shifts your physiology out of the fight-or-flight state. Thanks to mirror neurons, your smile is contagious; it sends a disarming message to others.

Observe

Observe what's actually happening, separate from your evaluation, and assess the TRIP.

Lengthen Your Spine

Shift your posture to align along your vertical axis. An upright posture activates the extensor muscles and counters the flexion associated with fight or flight.

Visualize

Visualize yourself as free, lengthening, and open. Soften your gaze to expand your peripheral vision. In the fight-or-flight pattern we tend to narrow the gaze.

Expand and Empathize

Expand your energy in a sphere around you. As you do, check in with your feelings and needs and attune to the feelings and needs of others.

To support you in your practice, I'm providing a link to a free page on my website where I will guide you in this practice and share a few more: www.michaelgelb.com. Once you get into the habit of centering, you'll find yourself doing it more frequently, as it feels good and is naturally self-reinforcing. The more you practice, the better it feels and the easier it is to do it when you really need it.

A New Respect

Aikido translates enlightened notions of interpersonal harmony into embodied experience. As you practice centering on your own, you'll want to experiment with the way you can actually blend with someone else's energy to create a deeper connection. Try this exercise:

Stand opposite a partner. (For beginners it's best to find
someone about your height and weight. As you get
more advanced, you can do this with people who are
much bigger and stronger.)

Your partner stands in a comfortable, balanced, upright
stance, with left foot forward, right foot back.

Stand facing your partner in a comfortable, balanced, upright stance, with left foot forward, right foot back.

Extend your right arm toward your partner as though you
were going to shake hands. Your partner grabs your
right wrist with his left hand and holds firmly.

Imagine a line drawn horizontally between you, and attempt
to pull your partner across the line onto your side. Your
partner's job is to resist without leaning back and to
hold firmly without letting go of your wrist. You'll discover that unless there's a gross disparity between your
strength and your partner's, you will not be able to pull
him across the line.

It's usually clear to both parties, and to witnesses, in a matter of seconds that you won't be able to move your partner this way. Ask your partner to let go, and both of you
take a minute to discuss what it feels like: for you to try
to force your partner across the line and for him as he
receives the force.

Now begin again. But this time, as your partner grabs your
wrist, focus on centering yourself. Instead of attempting to pull him across the line, relax your right elbow
so it sinks down and extend the energy from the back of
your wrist into your partner's grip. As your right elbow
sinks, allow your right index finger to float up so it's
pointing toward the sky in a spiral pattern. You'll notice
that your partner's left elbow is floating up.

Then, keeping your elbow and hand in line with the center line of your torso, pivot to your right. If your partner holds on, as he is supposed to, he will find that he's on your side of the line.

A few years ago I was teaching an introductory aikido class as part of a three-week residential leadership development and team-building program for a group of twenty-four international investment bankers. We discussed centering and blending in the seminar room and then moved to a dojo that they had built as part of their corporate university facility.

I invited the biggest and strongest-looking character in the class to help in the demonstration. He also happened to be the most senior member of the British division of the bank. When Paul, who looked like a fit version of Winston Churchill, grabbed my wrist in the first part of the demonstration, I was shocked by the viselike quality of his grip. There was no way I could budge him using my strength against his, and the smug, self-satisfied look on his face told me that he also knew this right away.

I said to the class, "Paul is a very powerful guy, and there's obviously no way I can get him over to my side using strength alone." They chuckled, and everyone, especially Paul, was sure that they were about to witness an embarrassing (for me) but amusing (for them) failed demonstration.

Here's what happened next. I said, "Paul, please grab my wrist again and hold even tighter. Just promise me you won't let go." He nodded and smirked. I continued, "I obviously can't move Paul with force, so instead I'm just going to connect with myself, with my own center, and as I do that I can feel Paul's center too."

I relaxed and dropped my elbow and floated my right index finger toward the ceiling. Paul's elbow drifted up.

"Now that I'm connected to Paul's center," I said, "let's see what happens if I turn around my central axis."

What happened? Paul not only came over to my side, but he seemed to float over like a ballerina. When he landed across the line, his look of utter astonishment was followed by a delightful quip that he shared in a voice just loud enough for the whole class to hear. He said, "I have a new respect for you."

Everyone laughed, and then I showed Paul how to bring me to his side by centering and blending. All of the investment bankers got the message. As the head of the U.S. branch commented, "I have always met aggression with more aggression. I usually win. But now I see there's a better way."

Epilogue

Wheels Down

n the past you had to be a billionaire to fly privately. Now, thanks to Wheels Up, you just need to be a CEO, EVP, athlete, media personality, or other successful professional to charter a plane to take you and your group wherever you want to go. Kenny Dichter explains that the power propelling the success of his venture is "people's desire to be together." A master of the common touch, he adds, "We treat a celebrity like a regular person and a regular person like a celebrity."

Wheels Down is the name of Dichter's events and concierge program that provides exciting opportunities for clients when they land, including parties around popular events like the Super Bowl, the Masters Golf Tournament, and Art Basel. But testimonials from their clients focus not so much on the experience of privilege and luxury, but rather on the benefit they experience from their ability to *connect more* with clients and family.

If you want to be healthier, happier, and live longer, if you want your career to take off, so that you *can* afford to fly privately, then practice the art of connection every day.

When you board a flight, you are always reminded that in case of difficulty, *put your oxygen mask on first, before assisting others.* In other words, connecting with your self allows you to connect more effectively with others. Embracing humility allows you to connect with a deeper aspect of yourself, beyond the ego. This awakens curiosity and allows others to feel that you are accessible and available to connect with them. You practice this every day by looking for the humanness, the soulfulness, in others (the common touch) and by cultivating the art of conversation.

Recognizing that emotions are contagious, you decide consciously what you want to catch and spread. You catch positive emotions and cultivate admirable qualities of character by constructively stalking great people and eliminating the deadbeats from your life. As you surround yourself with ever greater positive influences, you become a more positive influence yourself. You strengthen that positive leadership quality by consciously looking to bring out the best in others.

Training yourself to be free from slavery to likes and dislikes liberates you from the tyranny of constant evaluation, allowing you to cultivate discernment. In other words as you get more skilled at seeing things the way they are and as you free yourself from the habitual tendency to use evaluative language in your dealings with others, you are less likely to offend or stimulate defensive reactions and better able to build connections. Freedom from reflexive evaluation sets the stage for not taking everything quite so personally, and that makes it possible to evolve along the continuum of personal responsibility.

The three liberations generate tremendous positive energy that you can utilize for greater freedom: the freedom from slavery to your type and style. Apply the Costanza Principle and do the opposite to develop versatility. Versatility gives you many more options and skills with which to monitor and adjust the balance of energy exchange. Make the liberal exchange of SMART feedback and PRAISE part of your daily life, and although you expect the best from others, manage expectations wisely by consistently promising low and delivering high. Use creative thinking skills to anticipate and meet needs in the most efficient and creative manner, and practice full empathic (RARE) listening at least once a day.

Leadership is about meeting needs. The more senior leaders become, the greater the needs they are asked to address. Leaders monitor the balance of energy exchange and adjust it when necessary. Inevitably, conflicts arise. Growing as a leader requires the ability to be centered in the face of more complex challenges, so you can blend and discover creative solutions.

In the Introduction we learned that today's greatest organizations succeed by helping *all* their stakeholders thrive. They operate according to "radical new rules" such as: *Create partner relationships that really are mutually beneficial.* The seven relationship-building skills will help you awaken and champion mutual otherishness and I–Thou awareness, which make it possible to apply this rule. Use them to become an artist of connection, so you may realize your potential to lead us to a more creative, enlightened, and compassionate world.

Acknowledgments

hanks to all who contributed to the evolution of this book: Mark Andreas, Ed Bassett, J. G. Bennett, Ken Blanchard, Tony Buzan, Stephanie Cesario, Jim Clawson, Leslie "The Duck" Copland, Lorie Dechar, Kenny Dichter, Shoshana Dichter, Terry Dobson, Andrew Dornenburg, Jane Dutton, Gregg Fauceglia, Roger Fisher, Stasia Forsythe, Amy Fox, Mark Gayer, Marshall Goldsmith, Adam Grant, Forrest Hainline, Bob Hogan, Sam Horn, Russ Hudson, Marco Iacoboni, Brian Johnson, Jodie Katz, Grand Master Raymond Keene, Paula Kim, George Kohlreiser, David Lamb, Brian Lee, Quannah Lee, Dennis Mannion, Keith McFarland, Jack Meyer, Jon Miller, Anne Millikin, Riki Moss, Dinah Nieburg, Karen Page, Wendy Palmer, Belinda Parmar, Kevin Patterson, Dennis Perman, Chris Ranck, Pete Reilly, Mike Schwegman, Eva Selhub, Emma Seppälä, Evan Shepard, Raj Sisodia, Brandon Specktor, Rupert Spira, Gary Spitalnik, Michael Lee Stallard, Jack Stern, Rick Stickles, Bob Sutton, Robert Tangora, William Ury, Hank Weisinger, and Kathy Ziola. I am particularly grateful for the insights and inspiration provided by Marshall Rosenberg and his Center for Nonviolent Communication.

Thanks to the great team at New World Library: Jason Gardner, Monique Muhlenkamp, Munro Magruder, Kristen Cashman, Tona Pearce Myers, Tracy Cunningham, and Megan Colman. Thanks also to copyeditor Ann Moru.

Special thanks to: Deborah Domanski, Sandy and Joan Gelb, and Mort Herskowitz.

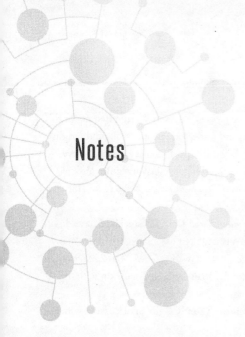

Notes

Prologue: Wheels Up

Page 1, *"We're probably the people"*: Gary Spitalnik, in discussion with the author, November 2016.

Page 2, *"Kenny Dichter is someone"*: Carly Okyle, "Meet Kenny Dichter, the 'Kevin Bacon' of Entrepreneurship," *Entrepreneur*, January 15, 2016.

Page 2, *"reflection of his gift for connecting"*: Shoshana Dichter, in discussion with the author, November 2016.

Page 2, *When you interact with any kind of organization*: Thanks to Professor Jim Clawson for these insights.

Page 3, *"Leadership is about managing energy"*: James Clawson, *Level Three Leadership: Getting Below the Surface*, 4th ed. (New York: Pearson, 2008), p. 3.

Page 6, *"This myth asserts that people simply"*: Warren Bennis, *Managing People Is like Herding Cats* (Cincinnati, OH: Covey Leadership Center, 1997), p. 163.

Page 7, *"I was a smart girl in a small town"*: Sam Horn, in discussion with the author, October 2016.

Page 7, *"You can make more friends"*: Dale Carnegie, *How to Win Friends and Influence People* (New York: Pocket Books, 1998), p. 52.

Page 7, *"Instead of talking about what I know"*: Horn, October 2016.

Page 7, *"Leadership is the art of accomplishing"*: Colin Powell, in Oren Harari, *The Leadership Secrets of Colin Powell* (New York: McGraw-Hill, 2002), p. 13.

Page 7, *Managers are busy cutting their way*: Thanks to Stephen Covey for introducing me to this metaphor.

Page 8, *In the past managers were asked to focus*: Thanks to Warren Bennis for this insight. Managers do things right, and leaders are people who do the right thing. Both roles are crucial, and they differ profoundly. I often observe people in top positions doing the wrong things well. Warren Bennis and Burt Nanus, *Leaders: The Strategies for Taking Charge* (New York: Harper & Row, 1985), p. 21.

Page 9, *Clawson refers to the attempt to manipulate*: Jim Clawson and I have discussed the material on his three levels and their associated principles many times over the last twelve years; see also Clawson, *Level Three Leadership*.

Page 11, *"One of my regular patients, Anita"*: Joan Gelb, in discussion with the author, September 2016.

Page 11, *"It wasn't part of my formal training"*: Sandy Gelb, in discussion with the author, September 2016.

Page 13, *"It ought to be remembered that there is nothing more perilous"*: Niccolò Machiavelli, *The Prince*, chap. 6, http://www.bartleby.com/36/1/prince.pdf.

Page 14, *"astonishing how elements which seem insoluble"*: Carl Rogers, *A Way of Being* (New York: Houghton Mifflin, 1980), p. 12.

Page 16, *"I quote others only"*: Michel de Montaigne, *Essais* (1595), book 1, chap. 26.

Page 17, *"You cannot live for yourselves"*: Henry Melvill, from a sermon entitled "Partaking in Other Men's Sins," given at St. Margaret's Church, Lothbury, England, June 12, 1855; printed in *Golden Lectures* (1855).

Introduction: The Secret of Health, Happiness, and Leadership

Page 21, *"A leader isn't good"*: Stanley McChrystal, "Listen, Learn...Then Lead," TED Talk, March 2011, https://www.ted.com/talks/stanley_mcchrystal?language=en.

Page 21, *"Everything went wrong"*: Mark Bowden, "The Desert One Debacle," *The Atlantic*, May 2006.

Page 22, *"the unrelenting demand for continual adaptability"*: McChrystal, "Listen, Learn...Then Lead."

Page 22, *"By the time you're a social worker"*: Brené Brown, "The Power of Vulnerability," TED Talk, June 2010, https://www.ted.com/talks/brene_brown_on_vulnerability?language=en.

Page 23, *most younger men believe that money*: Robert J. Waldinger, "What Makes a Good Life?: Lessons from the Longest Study on Happiness," TED Talk,

November 2015, https://www.ted.com/talks/robert_waldinger_what
_makes_a_good_life_lessons_from_the_longest_study_on_happiness
?language=en.

Page 23, *many research-validated benefits*: Emma Seppälä, http://www.emma
seppala.com, TEDxHayward; confirmed via direct communication with the
author, January 2017.

Page 24, *"My religion is kindness"*: The Dalai Lama, quoted in Gill Farrer-Halls,
*The World of the Dalai Lama: An Inside Look at His Life, His People, and His
Vision* (Wheaton, IL: Quest Books, 1998), p. 110.

Page 24, *E Pluribus Unum*: Michael Lee Stallard, in discussion with the author,
September 2016.

Page 26, *"To be honest, I really don't give a damn"*: Marco Iacoboni, in discussion
with the author, September 2016.

Page 27, *"Jane Goodall shared extraordinary stories"*: Iacoboni, September 2016.

Page 28, *"A wealth of information creates"*: Herbert A. Simon, "Designing
Organizations for an Information-Rich World," in Martin Greenberger,
ed., *Computers, Communication, and the Public Interest* (Baltimore: Johns
Hopkins Univ. Press, 1971), pp. 40–41.

Page 28, *"Men standing in opposite hemispheres"*: *The Notebooks of Leonardo da
Vinci*, vol. 2, trans. Jean Paul Richter (New York: Dover, 1970), p. 363.

Page 29, *"I think if we're all honest about it"*: Richard J. Davidson, in Carolyn
Gregoire, "Our Digital Device Addiction Is Causing a 'National Attention
Deficit,'" http://www.huffingtonpost.com/2014/10/03/neuroscientist
-richard-da_n_5923648.html.

Page 29, *"Is too much technology taking your body"*: Karen Grace, "'Tech Neck'
Taking a Toll on Child Posture," *USA Today*, http://www.usatoday.com
/story/news/health/2015/07/09/tech-neck-taking-a-toll-on-child
-posture/29905293.

Page 29, *"There's a pandemic of orthopedic ailments"*: Jack Stern, in discussion
with the author, September 2016.

Page 30, *"Rapport demands joint attention"*: Daniel Goleman, *Focus: The Hidden
Driver of Excellence* (New York: Harper Paperbacks, 2015), p. 7.

Page 30, *Zen Koans for the Internet Age*: Brandon Specktor, *Reader's Digest*,
http://www.rd.com/joke/zen-koans-for-the-internet-age. He graciously
granted permission to share these witticisms.

Page 30, *more than 50 percent of people on Facebook*: Sheryl Sandberg Facebook
post, January 21, 2016.

Page 31, *"live at the epicenter where the worlds"*: Jason Hirschhorn post, *Redef*, May 2016.

Page 31, *"even more disturbing"*: Nicholas Carr, *The Shallows: What the Internet Is Doing to Our Brains* (New York: Norton, 2011), 115.

Page 31, *"The Net seizes our attention"*: Carr, *The Shallows*, p. 118.

Page 32, *"I turn off the computer at dinnertime"*: Brian Johnson, in discussion with the author, October 2016.

Page 32, *"Twenty minutes of walking in the park"*: Eva Selhub, in discussion with the author, September 2016.

Page 33, *"Fix your course to a star"*: *Notebooks of Leonardo da Vinci*, vol. 1, p. 262.

Page 33, *"If you want to win the war for attention"*: David Brooks, "The Art of Focus," *New York Times*, June 2, 2014, https://www.nytimes.com/2014/06/03/opinion/brooks-the-art-of-focus.html.

Page 33, *our world was becoming increasingly impersonal*: Martin Buber, *I and Thou*, classic ed. (New York: Scribner, 2000).

Page 34, *"All real life is meeting"*: Buber, *I and Thou*, p. 26.

Page 34, *"I have to keep after some of the younger members"*: Gary Spitalnik, in discussion with the author, November 2016.

Page 34, *"I share a tremendous amount of information"*: Jon Miller, in discussion with the author, November 2016.

Page 35, *"underestimate the power of their persuasiveness"*: Vanessa K. Bohns, "A Face-to-Face Request Is 34 Times More Successful Than an Email," *Harvard Business Review*, April 11, 2017, https://hbr.org/2017/04/a-face-to-face-request-is-34-times-more-successful-than-an-email.

Page 35, *"Despite the reach of email"*: Vanessa K. Bohns, "A Face-to-Face Request."

Page 36, *today's greatest organizations succeed by helping*: Raj Sisodia, Jag Sheth, and David Wolfe, *Firms of Endearment: How World-Class Companies Profit from Passion and Purpose*, 2nd ed. (Upper Saddle River, NJ: Pearson Education, 2014).

Page 36, *The firms studied by Sisodia and his colleagues*: Raj Sisodia, in discussion with the author, October 2016.

Page 36, *"Create partner relationships"*: Sisodia, October 2016.

Page 36, *"Everything is connected"*: This is a paraphrase of Leonardo's statement "Everything comes from everything, and everything is made out of everything, and everything returns into everything." See Michael Gelb, *How to Think like Leonardo da Vinci* (New York: Delta Paperback, 2000), p. 226.

Page 36, *In the Buddhist scriptures, the* Avatamsaka Sutra: Thomas Cleary, *The Flower Ornament Scripture: A Translation of the Avatamsaka Sutra* (Boston: Shambhala, 1993).

Page 37, *"Finding the center of strength"*: Rollo May, *Man's Search for Himself* (1953; reprint, New York: Norton, 2009), p. 54.

Page 38, *"who works on his own development"*: Peter F. Drucker, *Management: Tasks, Responsibilities, Practices* (New York: Harper & Row, 1973), p. 427.

Page 38, *"Only the shallow know themselves"*: Oscar Wilde, *Epigrams: Phrases and Philosophies for the Use of the Young* (1882; reprint, Boston: C. C. Brainard, 1909), p. 142.

Page 38, *"Western business people often don't get"*: Daniel Goleman, in Perry Garfinkel, "Reconsidering, from the Heart," *Wall Street Journal*, April 25, 2012.

Chapter 1: Embrace Humility

Page 41, *"Do you wish to rise?"*: St. Augustine, Sermon on the New Testament 19:2.

Page 41, *Word-Association Exercise*: An earlier version of this material appeared in Michael J. Gelb, *Thinking for a Change* (New York: Crown, 1996), p. 137.

Page 43, *approximately 108 billion humans*: Carl Haub, "How Many People Have Ever Lived on Earth?," Population Reference Bureau, October 2011, http://www.prb.org/Publications/Articles/2002/HowManyPeople HaveEverLivedonEarth.aspx.

Page 43, *"Our research was able to isolate"*: Jeanine Prime and Elizabeth Salib, "The Best Leaders Are Humble Leaders," *Harvard Business Review*, May 12, 2014, https://hbr.org/2014/05/the-best-leaders-are-humble-leaders.

Page 44, *when a group of biochemists were challenged*: An earlier version of this material appeared in Gelb, *Thinking for a Change*.

Page 46, *subjects believed that the song they tapped*: Elizabeth Newton, "Overconfidence in the Communication of Intent: Heard and Unheard Melodies," PhD diss., Stanford University, 1990.

Page 46, *Psychologists call this phenomenon*: See, for example, Heidi Grant Halvorson, *No One Understands You and What to Do about It* (Boston: Harvard Business Review Press, 2015).

Page 47, *"I know that you believe"*: Robert McCloskey, at a press briefing referenced by Marvin Kalb, CBS reporter, in *TV Guide*, March 31, 1984.

Page 47, *What's the single greatest problem*: This question and its answer are based on this quote: "The single biggest problem in communication is the illusion that it has taken place." It is commonly attributed to George Bernard Shaw, but he didn't say it. According to Quote Investigator, the source is William Hollingsworth Whyte, "Is Anybody Listening?" *Fortune*, September 1950, p. 174.

Page 48, *"In a global marketplace where problems are"*: Prime and Salib, "The Best Leaders."

Page 48, *"The finest leaders are keenly aware"*: Bill George, "Are Our Leaders Losing Their Humility?," http://www.huffingtonpost.com/bill-george /are-our-leaders-losing-th_b_9423986.html.

Page 49, *humility is more than just a virtue*: Bradley P. Owens, Michael D. Johnson, and Terence R. Mitchell, "Expressed Humility in Organizations: Implications for Performance, Teams, and Leadership," *Organization Science* 4, no. 5 (September–October 2013): 1517–38.

Page 49, *cultivating humility "might just make us more effective"*: Foster School of Business, "Humility Is a Key to High Performance and Effective Leadership," September 19, 2012, http://foster.uw.edu/research-brief/humility -is-a-key-to-high-performance-and-effective-leadership.

Page 50, *"You become vulnerable. It's a paradox"*: Stephen R. Covey, *The 7 Habits of Highly Effective People: Powerful Lessons in Personal Change* (New York: Free Press, 1989), p. 243.

Page 50, *"vulnerability is the core, the heart"*: Brené Brown, *Daring Greatly: How the Courage to Be Vulnerable Transforms the Way We Live, Love, Parent, and Lead* (New York: Gotham, 2012), p. 13.

Page 50, *"It requires transparency"*: Adam Bryant, "Walt Bettinger of Charles Schwab: You've Got to Open Up to Move Up," *New York Times*, February 4, 2016, https://www.nytimes.com/2016/02/07/business/walt -bettinger-of-charles-schwab-youve-got-to-open-up-to-move-up.html ?_r=0.

Page 53, *"The armored, mechanistically rigid person"*: Wilhelm Reich, *Ether, God and Devil: Cosmic Superimposition* (New York: Macmillan, 2013), p. 10.

Page 53, *"Don't be so humble"*: Golda Meir, "Selected Quotes from Golda Meir," Golda Meir Center for Political Leadership, Metropolitan State University of Denver, http://www.msudenver.edu/golda/goldameir/goldaquotes.

Page 53, *"There is an affected humility"*: Arthur Martine, *Martine's Hand-book of Etiquette, and Guide to True Politeness* (1866), http://www.gutenberg.org /ebooks/36048. Summarized in Maria Popova, "The Art of Conversation:

Timeless, Timely Do's and Don'ts from 1866," Brain Pickings, https://www.brainpickings.org/2013/04/17/the-art-of-conversation -martine-etiquette-1866.

Page 55, *"Too often we underestimate the power"*: Leo F. Buscaglia, *Born for Love: Reflections on Loving* (New York: Ballantine Books, 1994), p. 232.

Page 56, *"Leaders can bring out the best"*: Jane Dutton, in discussion with the author, January 2017.

Page 57, *"Positive emotions compound quickly"*: Dutton, January 2017; see also Monica Worline and Jane Dutton, *Awakening Compassion at Work: The Quiet Power That Elevates People and Organizations* (Oakland, CA: Berrett-Koehler, 2017).

Page 58, *"If you can talk with crowds"*: Rudyard Kipling, from the poem "If," in *Rewards and Fairies* (New York: Doubleday, 1910).

Page 58, *"I've taught you everything I can teach you"*: Bryant, "Walt Bettinger of Charles Schwab."

Page 59, *A Master of the Common Touch*: Jack Meyer, in discussion with the author, September 2016.

Page 61, *"I speak to everyone in the same way"*: Alice Calaprice, *The New Quotable Einstein* (Princeton, NJ: Princeton University Press, 2005), p. 206.

Page 62, *"the most human and humanizing thing that we do"*: Sherry Turkle, on National Public Radio, September 26, 2015, NPR *Weekend Edition*.

Page 62, *an all-time classic guide to conversation*: Martine, *Martine's Hand-book of Etiquette, and Guide to True Politeness.*

Chapter 2: Be a Glowworm

Page 65, *"We are all worms"*: Fred R. Shapiro, *The Yale Book of Quotations* (New Haven, CT: Yale University Press, 2006), p. 155, where it is credited to Violet Bonham-Carter in *Winston Churchill as I Knew Him* (1965); see also https://www.nationalchurchillmuseum.org/winston-churchill-leadership -the-glow-worm.html.

Page 65, *"Flames seemed to whip hundreds of feet"*: Ernie Pyle, "Blitz: The City Ablaze," December 29, 1940, in H. R. Knickerbocker, *Is Tomorrow Hitler's?: 200 Questions on the Battle of Mankind* (New York: Reynal & Hitchcock, 1941), pp. 140, 150, 178–79.

Page 66, *When he was named prime minister*: Robert Self, *Neville Chamberlain: A Biography* (Farnham, UK: Ashgate, 2006), p. 431.

Page 66, *"Every man is like"*: Euripides, *Phoenix*, Frag. 809.

Page 67, *"computational social science"*: Nicholas A. Christakis and James H. Fowler, *Connected: The Surprising Power of Our Social Networks and How They Shape Our Lives* (Boston: Little, Brown, 2009); see also Nicholas Christakis, "Social Networks Are like the Eye" (2008), https://www.youtube.com/watch?v=3MjUstR1DzY.

Page 67, *"You are the average of the five people"*: Jim Rohn Facebook post, September 6, 2014, https://www.facebook.com/OfficialJimRohn/posts /10154545230540635.

Page 67, *"The amazing thing about social networks"*: Christakis, "Social Networks Are like the Eye."

Page 67, *"There is a lot of mirroring going on between people"*: Marco Iacoboni, in discussion with the author, September 2016.

Page 68, *Here's the conversation that ensued*: Mike Schwegman, in discussion with the author, June 2016.

Page 69, *"I literally would stalk people"*: Keith McFarland, in discussion with the author, October 2016.

Page 70, *"Really great people make you feel"*: The Quote Investigator attributes this to Mark Twain based on the memoir of Gay Zenola MacLaren. MacLaren was renowned for a superb memory, so the Quote Investigator believes it's valid; http://quoteinvestigator.com/2013/03/23/belittle -ambitions.

Page 70, *"Lives of great men all remind us"*: Henry Wadsworth Longfellow, "A Psalm of Life," http://www.poemhunter.com/poem/a-psalm-of-life.

Page 72, *"I know the term offends some people"*: Robert Sutton, "Why I Wrote the No Asshole Rule," *Harvard Business Review*, March 17, 2007, https://hbr.org/2007/03/why-i-wrote-the-no-asshole-rule; and in discussion with the author, February 2017.

Page 72, *"25 percent of managers who admitted"*: Christine Porath and Christine Pearson, "The Price of Incivility," *Harvard Business Review*, January– February 2013, https://hbr.org/2013/01/the-price-of-incivility.

Page 73, *"Even though there are occasions"*: Sutton, "Why I Wrote the No Asshole Rule."

Page 73, *"If I am walking with two other men"*: Confucius, *The Analects*, chap. 5.

Page 73, *Chris's Super Power*: Chris Ranck, in discussion with the author, September 2016.

Page 75, *"A man should never be appointed"*: Peter Drucker, *The Practice of Management* (1954; reprint, London: Routledge, 2012), p. 157.

Page 75, *a cadre of army drill sergeants were told*: X. Bezuijen, et al., "Pygmalion and Employee Learning: The Role of Leader Behaviors," *Journal of Management* 35, no. 5 (2009): 1248–67; doi:10.1177/0149206308329966.

Page 76, *"We have learned that when teachers"*: Robert Rosenthal, www.psychology .ucr.edu/faculty/rosenthal/index.html; see also Robert Rosenthal and Lenore Jacobson, *Pygmalion in the Classroom*, expanded ed. (New York: Irvington, 1992).

Page 77, *"It's not magic"*: Robert Rosenthal, quoted in Alix Spiegel, "Teachers' Expectations Can Influence How Students Perform," *NPR Morning Edition*, September 17, 2012.

Page 77, *What managers expect of subordinates*: J. Sterling Livingston, "Pygmalion in Management," *Harvard Business Review*, January 2003, https://hbr.org/2003/01/pygmalion-in-management.

Page 78, *"Treat a man as he is"*: Johann Wolfgang von Goethe; confirmed with Goethe scholar Raymond Keene.

Page 80, *"Do you want to meet the love of your life?"*: Byron Katie, *Question Your Thinking, Change the World* (Carlsbad, CA: Hay House, 2007), p. 30.

Page 80, *"Beauty is eternity gazing at itself"*: Kahlil Gibran, *The Prophet* (New York: Knopf, 1923), p. 76.

Page 80, *"realization of God's presence in oneself"*: Paramahansa Yogananda, *Autobiography of a Yogi*, https://www.yogananda-srf.org.

Chapter 3: Achieve the Three Liberations

Page 81, *"The contemplation of things"*: Francis Bacon, http://www.sirbacon.org /links/baconquotes.html.

Page 81, *"Overcoming like and dislike is the first practical step"*: John G. Bennett, *The First Liberation: Freedom from Like and Dislike*, Sherborne Theme Talks Series, No. 1 (Sherborne, Gloucestershire, UK: Coombe Springs Press, 1976).

Page 83, *"J. Krishnamurti once remarked"*: Marshall Rosenberg, *Nonviolent Communication: A Language of Life*, 2nd ed. (Encinitas, CA: PuddleDancer Press, 2003), p. 28.

Page 84, *Let's explore the difference*: Rosenberg, *Nonviolent Communication*, p. 34.

Page 86, *Marshall Rosenberg explains*: Marshall B. Rosenberg, PhD, *Raising Children Compassionately: Parenting the Nonviolent Communication Way*

(Encinitas, CA: PuddleDancer Press, 2005), p. 1; also available at
https://www.cnvc.org/Raising-Children-Compassionately.

Page 87, *"If you can't say something good"*: According to the Quote Investigator,
this quip first appeared as embroidery on a pillow displayed prominently
in the sitting room of Alice Roosevelt Longworth (1884–1980),
http://quoteinvestigator.com/category/alice-roosevelt-longworth.

Page 87, *"Patience serves us against insults"*: *The Notebooks of Leonardo da Vinci*,
vol. 2, trans. Jean Paul Richter (New York: Dover, 1970), p. 298.

Page 88, *"When a wind of personal reaction comes"*: Rumi, in Coleman Barks,
The Essential Rumi (San Francisco: HarperOne, 2004), p. 224.

Page 89, *"He actually shouted at me"*: Quannah Lee, in discussion with the author, September 2016.

Page 89, *"When you're twenty"*: This remark is usually attributed to Winston
Churchill, but there's no evidence that he ever said it.

Page 89, *"Well, perhaps one has to be very old"*: Pearl S. Buck, *China Past and
Present* (New York: John Day, 1972), chap. 6.

Page 90, *"Misunderstandings and neglect create more confusion"*: Johann
Wolfgang von Goethe; confirmed with Goethe scholar Raymond Keene.

Page 90, *"Nothing other people do"*: Don Miguel Ruiz, *The Four Agreements:
A Practical Guide to Personal Wisdom* (San Rafael, CA: Amber-Allen,
1997), p. 50.

Page 91, *"Leadership consists of nothing but"*: Dwight D. Eisenhower, in Edgar
F. Puryear Jr., *Nineteen Stars: A Study in Military Character and Leadership*
(1971; reprint, Novato, CA: Presidio Press, 1981), p. 289.

Page 92, *"The price of greatness"*: Winston Churchill, speech at Harvard
University, September 6, 1943, http://www.winstonchurchill.org
/resources/speeches/1941-1945-war-leader/420-the-price-of-greatness
-is-responsibility.

Page 92, *"Every thought, every word"*: Aung San Suu Kyi, Nobel lecture, Oslo,
Norway, June 16, 2012, http://www.nobelprize.org/nobel_prizes/peace
/laureates/1991/kyi-lecture_en.html.

Page 92, *"The central fact [is] that we"*: J. Krishnamurti, "Freedom from
the Known," http://www.jkrishnamurti.org/krishnamurti-teachings
/view-text.php?tid=48&chid=56784.

Page 92, *"There is no guide, no teacher"*: Krishnamurti, "Freedom from the
Known."

Page 93, *"One of the annoying things about believing"*: P. J. O'Rourke, *Rolling Stone*, November 30, 1989.

Page 93, *"I've always felt secretly guilty"*: Melanie Greenberg, "Why We Can't Stop Watching 'The Real Housewives,'" *Psychology Today*, https://www.psychologytoday.com/blog/the-mindful-self-express /201303/why-we-cant-stop-watching-the-real-housewives.

Page 94, *"A writer — and, I believe, generally all persons"*: Jorge Luis Borges, quoted in *Twenty-Four Conversations with Borges, Including a Selection of Poems: Interviews by Roberto Alifano, 1981–1983* (Housatonic, MA: Lascaux, 1984), p. 15.

Page 94, *"When people feel their insignificance"*: Rollo May, *Psychology and the Human Dilemma* (New York: Norton, 1967), p. 31.

Page 95, *"My job stinks"*: Dom Irrera, http://www.domirrera.com.

Page 95, *the average person complains once every minute*: Travis Bradberry, "How Complaining Rewires Your Brain for Negativity," *Entrepreneur*, September 9, 2016, https://www.entrepreneur.com/article/281734. (There's some question about the sources that Bradberry relies upon for this assertion. There are lots of complaints about it on the internet!)

Page 95, *people are interrupted after eighteen seconds*: H. B. Beckman and R. M. Frankel, "The Effect of Physician Behavior on the Collection of Data," *Annals of Internal Medicine* 101, no. 5 (November 1984): 692–96. This is a study of interruptions of patients by physicians.

Page 95, *Indulging in or colluding with whining*: Robert Sapolsky, "New Studies of Human Brains Show Stress May Shrink Neurons," *Stanford News Service*, August 14, 1996, http://news.stanford.edu/pr/96/960814shrnkgbrain.html.

Page 100, *"Everything we do is in service"*: Marshall B. Rosenberg, PhD, *Speak Peace in a World of Conflict: What You Say Next Will Change Your World* (Encinitas, CA: PuddleDancer Press, 2005), p. 10.

Chapter 4: Transcend Fixations

Page 103, *"Ultimately, the objective is"*: Dennis Perman, in discussion with the author, January 2017.

Page 105, *"We cannot safely assume"*: Isabel Briggs Myers and Peter Myers, *Gifts Differing: Understanding Personality Type* (Mountain View, CA: Davies-Black, 1980), p. 1.

Page 105, *"all the types suck"*: Dennis Perman, in discussion with the author, January 2017.

Page 106, *"Our type is not our identity"*: Russ Hudson, in discussion with the author, February 2017.

Page 108, *Supporting Compassion, Collaboration, and Connection*: Leslie Copland, in discussion with the author, February 2017.

Page 111, *"The differences between healthy, average, and unhealthy expressions"*: Russ Hudson, in discussion with the author, February 2017.

Page 111, *"Depending on the circumstance"*: Morihei Ueshiba, trans. John Stevens, *The Art of Peace* (Boston: Shambhala, 1992), p. 109.

Page 112, *the relative effectiveness of six different leadership styles*: Daniel Goleman, "Leadership That Gets Results," *Harvard Business Review*, March–April 2000, https://hbr.org/2000/03/leadership-that-gets-results.

Page 116, *"Being a Pacesetter is part of the job"*: Dennis Mannion, in discussion with the author, September 2016.

Page 119, *"that the realm of their inferior function"*: Marie-Louise von Franz, *Psychotherapy* (Boston: Shambhala, 2001), p. 34.

Page 120, *"I was the CEO of a technology company"*: Keith McFarland, in discussion with the author, October 2016.

Chapter 5: Balance Energy Exchange

Page 121, *"When we quit thinking"*: Joseph Campbell, with Bill Moyers, *The Power of Myth* (New York: Anchor, 1991), p. 31.

Page 123, *Grant divides people into three categories*: Adam Grant, *Give and Take: Why Helping Others Drives Our Success* (New York: Penguin, 2014); "Are You a Giver or a Taker?" TED Talk, November 2016, https://www.ted.com/talks/adam_grant_are_you_a_giver_or_a_taker.

Page 125, *"There is no meaningful 'yes'"*: Rollo May, *Power and Innocence* (New York: Norton, 1972), chap. 11.

Page 125, *The Power of a Positive No*: William Ury, *The Power of a Positive No* (New York: Bantam, 2007); "Say No and Still Get to Yes," https://www.youtube.com/watch?v=CDP2Ky_ypVo.

Page 125, *"Focusing is about saying 'no'"*: Steve Jobs, in Jonathan Becher, "6 Quotes to Help You Understand Why It's Important to Say No," http://www.forbes.com/sites/sap/2015/08/12/quotes-on-saying-no/#42eec4a27a7d3ee781a17a7d.

Page 125, *"The art of leadership"*: Tony Blair, *Daily Mail*, October 2, 1994.

Page 126, *She invites us to imagine this scene*: Sam Horn, in discussion with the author, September 2016.

Page 127, *"Never promise more"*: Publilius Syrus, *Sententiae*, Maxim 358.

Page 127, *"Always be impeccable with your word"*: Don Miguel Ruiz, *The Four Agreements: A Practical Guide to Personal Wisdom* (San Rafael, CA: Amber-Allen, 1997), p. 26.

Page 128, *"When people ask me what I do for a living"*: Kevin Patterson, in discussion with the author, November 2016.

Page 129, *"People know that if they announce"*: Raphael Malveau and Thomas Mowbray, *Software Architect Bootcamp* (Upper Saddle River, NJ: Prentice Hall, 2001), p. 258.

Page 129, *"People would come into my shop"*: Robert Tangora, in discussion with the author, January 2017.

Page 130, *"I think it's very important to have a feedback loop"*: Elon Musk, in John Brandon, "Elon Musk on How to Innovate: 20 Quotes," *Inc.*, July 14, 2015, http://www.inc.com/john-brandon/elon-musk-on-how-to-innovate-20-quotes.html.

Page 132, *calls feedback the "breakfast of champions"*: Kenneth Blanchard and Spencer Johnson, *The One Minute Manager* (New York: Berkley, 1983), p. 67.

Page 132, *SMART Feedback*: An earlier version of this material appeared in Michael J. Gelb, *Thinking for a Change* (New York: Crown, 1996).

Page 133, *"Response to a stimulus (such as criticism or praise)"*: *Business Dictionary*, definition of *feedback*, http://www.businessdictionary.com/definition/feedback.html#ixzz41fAyJd1X.

Page 135, *"Honesty is not greater"*: Samuel Johnson, *The Beauties of Samuel Johnson: Maxims and Observations* (London: 1804), p. 192.

Page 135, *"the ability to tell someone to go to hell"*: This remark is usually attributed to Winston Churchill, but there's no evidence that he ever said this.

Page 136, *"Most people break out in a sweat"*: Hendrie "Hank" Weisinger, in discussion with the author, September 2016.

Page 137, *"You can tell the character of every man"*: Lucius Annaeus Seneca, *Letters from a Stoic* (London: Dover, 2016), p. 121.

Page 138, *"catching people doing something right"*: Blanchard and Johnson, *One Minute Manager*, p. 39.

Page 138, *"People who feel good about themselves"*: Blanchard and Johnson, *One Minute Manager*, p. 19.

Page 138, *"Nothing is more effective"*: Bill Walsh, "The Case for Kudos," *Forbes* 154, no. 8 (October 10, 1994): 13.

Page 139, *"You do ill if you praise"*: *The Notebooks of Leonardo da Vinci*, vol. 2, trans. Jean Paul Richter (New York: Dover, 1970), p. 299.

Page 139, *"Praise out of season"*: Pearl S. Buck, "First Meeting" in *To My Daughters, With Love* (New York: John Day, 1967), p. 48.

Page 139, *in a social setting a compliment about hairstyle*: Janie Rees-Miller, "Compliments Revisited: Contemporary Compliments and Gender," *Journal of Pragmatics* 43 (2011): 2673–88.

Page 139, *"The love of praise"*: Edward Young, *The Love of Fame*, Satire I, line 51.

Page 140, *"There are two things people want"*: Mary Kay Ash, in Michael LeBoeuf, *The Greatest Management Principle in the World* (New York: Putnam, 1985), p. 97.

Page 140, *shared an interaction she had recently*: Chris Ranck, in discussion with the author, September 2016.

Page 141, *"You must go on trying to be sincere"*: G. I. Gurdjieff, *Views from the Real World: Early Talks of Gurdjieff as Recollected by his Pupils* (New York: Dutton, 1973), p. 145.

Page 141, *"My mother's words became"*: Commonly attributed to Mary Kay Ash.

Page 144, *"Leaders know the importance"*: Warren Bennis, *On Becoming a Leader*, 4th ed. (New York: Basic Books, 2009), p. 190.

Page 144, *"When I became an executive coach"*: Marshall Goldsmith, in discussion with the author, January 2017.

Page 145, *"developing leaders who make a positive"*: "Michigan Ross to Launch Leadership Center with $20 Million Gift from Former General Mills CEO Stephen Sanger and Karen Sanger," https://michiganross.umich.edu/news/u-michigan-launch-leadership-center-20-million-gift-former-general-mills-ceo-stephen-sanger-and.

Page 145, *"Who is the happiest of men?"*: Johann Wolfgang von Goethe; confirmed with Goethe scholar Raymond Keene.

Chapter 6: Be A RARE Listener

Page 149, *"Everything that needs to be said"*: André Gide, in Marcus Herzig, *Memoirs of a Johnny's Fanboy* (Bochum, Germany: Boysterous Books, 2012), p. 5.

Page 149, *"Ever notice that anyone going slower"*: George Carlin, "Idiot and Maniac," https://www.youtube.com/watch?v=XWPCE2tTLZQ; *Napalm and Silly Putty* (New York: Hyperion, 2001).

Page 150, *"people who lack the knowledge or wisdom"*: Justin Kruger and David Dunning, "Unskilled and Unaware of It: How Difficulties in Recognizing One's Own Incompetence Lead to Inflated Self-Assessments," *Journal of Personality and Social Psychology* 77, no. 6 (December 1999): 1121–34.

Page 150, *"Are we all less risky"*: Ola Svenson, "Are We All Less Risky and More Skillful Than Our Fellow Drivers?" *Acta Psychologica* 47, no. 2 (February 1981): 143–48; doi:10.1016/0001-6918(81)90005-6.

Page 150, *people often overestimate their popularity*: Tori DeAngelis, "Why We Overestimate Our Competence," *Monitor on Psychology* 34, no. 2 (February 2003), American Psychological Association, http://www.apa.org/monitor/feb03/overestimate.aspx.

Page 151, *89 percent of Americans admit*: Sherry Turkle, "Stop Googling. Let's Talk," *New York Times*, September 26, 2015, https://www.nytimes.com/2015/09/27/opinion/sunday/stop-googling-lets-talk.html.

Page 152, *"As a coach, a parent, or a leader"*: Mike Krzyzewski, CoachK.com, "Quotes," http://coachk.com/keywords-for-success/.

Page 153, *"Many of you have already heard a lot of advice"*: Celeste Headlee, "10 Ways to Have a Better Conversation," TEDxCreativeCoast, May 2015, https://www.ted.com/talks/celeste_headlee_10_ways_to_have_a_better_conversation.

Page 153, *The AI Rule*: Keith McFarland, in discussion with the author, November 2016.

Page 156, *"The curious paradox is that"*: Carl Rogers, *On Becoming a Person* (1961; reprint, Boston: Houghton Mifflin, 1995), p. 17.

Page 156, *"The more we hear them"*: Marshall Rosenberg, *Nonviolent Communication: A Language of Life*, 2nd ed. (Encinitas, CA: PuddleDancer Press, 2003), p. 150.

Page 157, *"I'm against picketing"*: Mitch Hedberg, from his album *Strategic Grill Locations*, https://www.youtube.com/watch?v=tE6Wkm3aVKA.

Page 157, *"It is with the heart that one sees"*: Antoine de Saint-Exupéry, *The Little Prince*, chap. 21.

Page 158, *whatever the psychotherapeutic style, one-third*: R. Elliott, et al., "Empathy," *Psychotherapy* (Chicago) 48, no. 1 (March 2011): 43–49; doi:10.1037/a0022187.

Page 159, *"You might fear it will make you"*: Heidi Grant Halvorson, quoted in Stephanie Vozza, "How the Most Successful People Ask Questions," *Fast Company*, February 8, 2016, https://www.fastcompany.com/3056318/how -the-most-successful-people-ask-questions.

Page 161, *"Remember not only to say the right thing"*: Benjamin Franklin, in *The Pennsylvania Gazette*, 1754.

Page 161, *"Never miss a good chance"*: Will Rogers, "The Manly Wisdom of Will Rogers," in Nina Colman, *The Friars Club Bible of Jokes, Pokes, Roasts, and Toasts* (New York: Black Dog & Leventhal, 2001), p. 316.

Page 161, *"Let a fool hold his tongue"*: Publilius Syrus, *Sententiae*, Maxim 914.

Page 161, *"But far more numerous was the herd"*: John Dryden, *Absalom and Achitophel* (1681), Part. I, lines 532–33.

Page 162, *"Leaders show respect for people"*: Mike Krzyzewski, CoachK.com, "Quotes," http://coachk.com/quotes.

Page 163, *"My friends tell me I have an intimacy problem"*: Garry Shandling, blog, March 24, 2016, http://childoftelevision.blogspot.com/2016/03/garry -shandling.html.

Page 163, *Well-meaning people often rely*: Adapted from and inspired by Rosenberg, *Nonviolent Communication*, p. 92.

Page 164, *In this exercise, based on the work of Marshall Rosenberg*: Adapted from and inspired by Rosenberg, *Nonviolent Communication*, pp. 109–11.

Page 167, *"I don't mean to interrupt"*: Paula Poundstone, *Wait, Wait...Don't Tell Me*, National Public Radio.

Page 167, *proclaimed our era the "Age of Interruption"*: Thomas Friedman, "The Age of Interruption," *New York Times*, July 5, 2006.

Page 169, *the top 5 percent, as ranked by colleagues*: Jack Zenger and Joseph Folkman, "What Great Listeners Actually Do," *Harvard Business Review*, July 14, 2016, https://hbr.org/2016/07/what-great-listeners-actually-do.

Page 171, *skill in understanding others accurately*: William Ickes, *Everyday Mind Reading: Understanding What Other People Think and Feel* (New York: Prometheus, 2003).

Page 172, *The research-validated benefits*: M. A. Stewart, "Effective Physician-Patient Communication and Health Outcomes: A Review," *Canadian Medical Association Journal* 152, no. 9 (1995): 1423–33; Amol Utrankar and Elaine Ecklund, "Empathy in the Physician-Patient Relationship: How Physicians Define, Develop, and Demonstrate Emotional Work in Clinical Practice,"

December 13, 2012, https://scholarship.rice.edu/bitstream/handle
/1911/70918/Utrankar_Research-Paper.pdf?sequence=2.

Page 173, *"In medical school we were told"*: Jodie Katz, in discussion with the author, February 2017.

Page 175, *"I do know one reason why I'm successful"*: Kevin Dutton and Andy McNab, *The Good Psychopath's Guide to Success* (Malmsbury, UK: Apostrophe, 2014), p. 16.

Page 175, *Good psychopaths, according to the authors*: Dutton and McNab, *The Good Psychopath's Guide*. For a test that allows you to assess your psychopathic tendencies, go to http://www.thegoodpsychopath.com.

Page 175, *"The key idea is that we all lie somewhere"*: Simon Baron-Cohen, *Zero Degrees of Empathy: A New Theory of Human Cruelty* (London: Allen Lane, 2011), p. 10. For an empathy quotient test developed by Simon Baron-Cohen at the Autism Research Centre at the University of Cambridge, go to https://psychology-tools.com/empathy-quotient.

Page 175, *overreliance on feelings of empathy*: Paul Bloom, *Against Empathy* (New York: Ecco, 2016).

Page 176, *"Altruistic intentions must be run through the sieve"*: Barbara A. Oakley, "Concepts and Implications of Altruism Bias and Pathological Altruism," *Proceedings of the National Academy of Sciences USA* 110, Suppl. 2 (June 18, 2013): 10408–15.

Page 176, *an empathy deficit*: Belinda Parmar, in discussion with the author, January 2017; see also http://www.theempathybusiness.co.uk.

Page 178, *"You're looking at another being"*: Ram Dass, "Love Is the Most Powerful Medicine," July 19, 2011, https://www.ramdass.org/love-is-the-most-powerful-medicine.

Page 178, *"Your sensing mechanism in life"*: Ram Dass, "Seeing Yourself in Another," November 17, 2016, https://www.ramdass.org/seeing-yourself-in-another.

Page 179, *"increased feelings of social connection and positivity"*: Emma Seppälä, "18 Science-Based Reasons to Try Loving-Kindness Meditation Today!," http://www.emmaseppala.com/18-science-based-reasons-try-loving-kindness-meditation-today.

Page 179, *"is effective in both immediate and small doses"*: C. A. Hutcherson, E. M. Seppälä, and J. J. Gross, "Loving-Kindness Meditation Increases Social Connectedness," *Emotion* 8, no. 5 (October 2008): 720–24; doi:10.1037/a0013237.

Page 180, *Six Scientifically Validated Benefits of LKM*: Emma Seppälä, "18

Science-Based Reasons to Try Loving-Kindness Meditation Today!"
http://www.emmaseppala.com/18-science-based-reasons-try-loving
-kindness-meditation-today/.

Chapter 7: Turn Friction into Momentum

Page 183, *"Anyone can hold the helm"*: Publilius Syrus, *Sententiae*, Maxim 358.

Page 183, *"I would not waste my life"*: Frances E. Willard, *Glimpses of Fifty Years: The Autobiography of an American Woman* (Chicago: Woman's Temperance Publishing Association, 1889), p. 231.

Page 185, *"It's just a job"*: Muhammad Ali, in Joyce Maynard, "Life with Ali: In a Neutral Corner," *New York Times*, April 6, 1977.

Page 185, *"An association of men who will not quarrel"*: Thomas Jefferson, letter to John Taylor, Philadelphia, PA, June 4, 1798, https://founders.archives
.gov/documents/Jefferson/01-30-02-0280.

Page 186, *"Conflict is the gadfly"*: John Dewey, ed. Jo Ann Boydston, *The Middle Works of John Dewey 1899–1924*, vol. 14: *Human Nature and Conduct* (Carbondale: Southern Illinois University Press, 1983), p. 207.

Page 186, *Conflict is the "oxygen" of creativity*: Sy Landau, Barbara Landau, and Daryl Landau, *From Conflict to Creativity: How Resolving Workplace Disagreements Can Inspire Innovation and Productivity* (San Francisco: Jossey-Bass, 2001), p. 87.

Page 187, *these companies promote diversity, collaboration*: Linda Hill et al., *Collective Genius: The Art and Practice of Leading Innovation* (Boston: Harvard Business Review Press, 2014).

Page 187, *"Creative abrasion is about having heated"*: Linda Hill, in Gareth Cook, "How to Manage a Creative Organization," *Scientific American*, October 21, 2014.

Page 187, *"Because all ideas pass through similar cognitive screens"*: Dorothy Leonard and Susaan Straus, "Putting Your Company's Whole Brain to Work," *Harvard Business Review*, July–August 1997, https://hbr.org
/1997/07/putting-your-companys-whole-brain-to-work.

Page 189, *"You can't make your kids"*: Marshall Rosenberg, *Nonviolent Communication: A Language of Life*, 2nd ed. (Encinitas, CA: PuddleDancer Press, 2003), p. 22.

Page 190, *"If a couple's negative events are not fully processed"*: Ellie Lisitsa, "The Zeigarnik Effect," *Gottman Relationship Blog*, August 15, 2012,

https://www.gottman.com/blog/what-makes-love-last-the-zeigarnik
-effect.

Page 190, *Most conflicts happen between people*: Nicholas A. Christakis and James
H. Fowler, *Connected: The Surprising Power of Our Social Networks and How
They Shape Our Lives* (Boston: Little, Brown, 2009), p. 5.

Page 191, *"Never wrestle with pigs"*: This remark is usually attributed to George
Bernard Shaw, but there's no evidence that he said it.

Page 191, *"Reprove a friend in private"*: *The Notebooks of Leonardo da Vinci*, vol.
2, trans. Jean Paul Richter (New York: Dover, 1970), p. 297.

Page 192, *"to respond personally"*: Roger Fisher and William Ury, *Getting to YES:
Negotiating Agreement Without Giving In* (New York: Penguin, 1991), p. 61.

Page 192, *"We had a serious dispute"*: Evan Shepard, in discussion with the author, September 2016.

Page 194, *"One should be in harmony"*: Bruce Lee, *Striking Thoughts: Bruce Lee's
Wisdom for Daily Living*, ed. John Little (Boston: Tuttle, 2000), part 2, p. 20.

Page 195, *"I felt the universe suddenly quake"*: Morihei Ueshiba, in Morihiro Saito,
Traditional Aikido, vol. 1 (Tokyo: Minato, 1973), p. 38.

Page 197, *"Aikido is ultimately"*: Wendy Palmer, in discussion with the author,
January 2017.

Page 198, *"In all forms of strategy, it is necessary"*: Miyamoto Musashi, *The Book
of Five Rings* (*The Water Book*), trans. Thomas Cleary (Boston: Shambhala,
2005), p. 27, http://www.bookoffiverings.com/WaterBook.htm.

Page 198, *"amygdala hijack"*: Dennis Hughes, "Interview with Daniel
Goleman," *Share Guide*, http://www.shareguide.com/Goleman.html.

Page 199, *"When angry, count to ten"*: Henry S. Randall, *The Life of Thomas
Jefferson*, vol. 3 (New York: Derby & Jackson, 1858), p. 525, https://www
.monticello.org/site/research-and-collections/famous-jefferson-quotes.

Page 201, *"A Kind Word Turneth Away Wrath"*: Riki Moss, Terry's partner, gra-
ciously granted permission for the adaptation of the story that appears here.
See also Terry Dobson and Victor Miller, *Giving In to Get Your Way: The
Attack-tics System for Winning Your Everyday Battles* (New York: Delacorte,
1978); Riki Moss with Terry Dobson, *An Obese White Gentleman in No
Apparent Distress* (Berkeley, CA: Blue Snake Books, 2009), a novel based
on the writings and recordings of Terry Dobson; and Morihei Ueshiba,
Aikido and the New Warrior, ed. R. S. Heckler (Berkeley, CA: North Atlantic
Books, 1985).

Page 205, *"I've just entered the hospital treatment room"*: George Kohlreiser, in discussion with the author, June 2016.

Page 208, *"Several years ago, I watched"*: Pete Reilly, in discussion with the author, April 2017.

Page 209, *"We were being sued by a fellow"*: Evan Shepard, in discussion with the author, November 2016.

Page 211, *"The ability to see the situation"*: Fisher and Ury, *Getting to YES*, p. 23.

Page 211, *"It is not enough to study them"*: Fisher and Ury, *Getting to YES*, p. 23.

Page 211, *"The more quickly you can turn a stranger"*: Fisher and Ury, *Getting to YES*, p. 37.

Page 212, *"Invent several options all equally acceptable"*: Fisher and Ury, *Getting to YES*, p. 75.

Page 212, *Mark Andreas spent seven years*: Mark Andreas, in discussion with the author, March 2017.

Page 213, *One of the legendary stories from the early days of the dojo*: Oral transmission.

Page 214, *The study concluded that*: B. Grayson and M. I. Stein, "Attracting Assault: Victims' Nonverbal Cues," *Journal of Communication* 31, no. 1 (1981): 68–75; Angela Book, Kimberly Costello, and Joseph A. Camilleri, "Psychopathy and Victim Selection: The Use of Gait as a Cue to Vulnerability," *Journal of Interpersonal Violence* 28, no. 11 (February 2013); doi: 10.1177/0886260512475315.

Epilogue: Wheels Down

Page 221, *"people's desire to be together"*: Kenny Dichter, in discussion with the author, March 2017.

Recommended Reading and Resources

A number of the authors listed below have written many excellent books. I've listed just one from each to get you started.

Mark Andreas, *Sweet Fruit from the Bitter Tree: 61 Stories of Creative and Compassionate Ways out of Conflict*, www.markandreas.com.

J. G. Bennett, *A Spiritual Psychology*, www.jgbennett.org.

Kenneth Blanchard and Spencer Johnson, *The One Minute Manager*, www.kenblanchard.com.

Brené Brown, *Daring Greatly: How the Courage to Be Vulnerable Transforms the Way We Live, Love, Parent, and Lead*, http://brenebrown.com.

Martin Buber, *I and Thou*.

The Catalyst Research Center for Advancing Leader Effectiveness, www.catalyst.org/knowledge/research-centers/advancing-leader-effectiveness.

James Clawson, *Level Three Leadership: Getting Below the Surface*.

Leslie Copland, www.lesliecoplandleadership.com.

Jane E. Dutton and Gretchen M. Spreitzer, eds., *How to Be a Positive Leader: Small Actions, Big Impact*, http://webuser.bus.umich.edu/janedut.

Roger Fisher and William Ury, *Getting to YES*, www.pon.harvard.edu.

Erica A. Fox, *Winning from Within: A Breakthrough Method for Leading, Living, and Lasting Change*, www.mobiusleadership.com.

Marshall Goldsmith and Mark Reiter, *Triggers: Creating Behavior That Lasts —
Becoming the Person You Want to Be*, http://marshallgoldsmithgroup.com.

Daniel Goleman, *Emotional Intelligence: Why It Can Matter More Than IQ*,
www.danielgoleman.info.

John Gottman and Nan Silver, *The Seven Principles for Making Marriage Work*,
www.gottman.com.

Adam Grant, *Give and Take: Why Helping Others Drives Our Success*,
www.adamgrant.net.

Morton Herskowitz, *Emotional Armoring: An Introduction to Psychiatric Orgone
Therapy*, www.orgonomicscience.org/emotional-armoring.

Sam Horn, *Tongue Fu!: How to Deflect, Disarm, and Defuse Any Verbal Conflict*,
www.samhorn.com.

Marco Iacoboni, *Mirroring People: The Science of Empathy and How We Connect
with Others*, http://iacoboni.bol.ucla.edu.

Brian Johnson, *A Philosopher's Notes: On Optimal Living, Creating an
Authentically Awesome Life and Other Such Goodness*, www.optimize.me
/philosophersnotes.

Dave Kerpen, *The Art of People: 11 Simple People Skills That Will Get You
Everything You Want*, www.davekerpen.ceo.

George Kohlrieser, *Hostage at the Table: How Leaders Can Overcome Conflict,
Influence Others, and Raise Performance*, www.georgekohlrieser.com.

J. Krishnamurti, *Freedom from the Known*, www.jkrishnamurti.org/index.php.

Rollo May, *Man's Search for Himself*, www.questia.com/library/104825219
/man-s-search-for-himself.

Stanley McChrystal, *Team of Teams: New Rules of Engagement for a Complex
World*, https://mcchrystalgroup.com.

Keith McFarland, *The Breakthrough Company: How Everyday Companies Become
Extraordinary Performers*, www.breakthroughcompany.com.

Wendy Palmer and Janet Crawford, *Leadership Embodiment: How the Way We
Sit and Stand Can Change the Way We Think and Speak*, www.embodiment
international.com.

Belinda Parmar, www. theempathybusiness.co.uk.

Dennis Perman, www.themasterscircle.com/Home.aspx.

Christine Porath, *Mastering Civility: A Manifesto for the Workplace*, www
.christineporath.com.

Baba Ram Dass, *Be Here Now*, www.ramdass.org.

Chris Ranck and Christopher Lee Nutter, *Ignite the Genius Within: Discover Your Full Potential*, www.christineranck.com.

Pete Reilly, *In the Garden of Hearts: Meditations, Consolations, and Blessings for Teachers*, www.petereilly.org.

Don Richard Riso and Russ Hudson, *The Wisdom of the Enneagram: The Complete Guide to Psychological and Spiritual Growth for the Nine Personality Types*, www.enneagraminstitute.com.

Carl Rogers, *On Becoming a Person: A Therapist's View of Psychotherapy.*

Marshall Rosenberg, *Nonviolent Communication: A Language of Life*, 2nd ed., www.cnvc.org.

Don Miguel Ruiz, *The Four Agreements: A Practical Guide to Personal Wisdom*, www.miguelruiz.com.

Eva Selhub, with Divina Infusino, *The Love Response: Your Prescription to Turn Off Fear, Anger, and Anxiety to Achieve Vibrant Health and Transform Your Life*, www.drselhub.com.

Emma Seppälä, *The Happiness Track: How to Apply the Science of Happiness to Accelerate Your Success*, www.emmaseppala.com.

Raj Sisodia, Jag Sheth, and David Wolfe, *Firms of Endearment: How World-Class Companies Profit from Passion and Purpose*, www.rajsisodia.com.

Michael Lee Stallard, *Connection Culture: The Competitive Advantage of Shared Identity, Empathy, and Understanding at Work*, www.michaelleestallard.com.

Robert Sutton, *The No Asshole Rule: Building a Civilized Workplace and Surviving One That Isn't*, http://bobsutton.typepad.com.

William Ury, *The Power of a Positive No: Save the Deal, Save the Relationship, and Still Say No*, www.williamury.com.

Robert Waldinger, http://robertwaldinger.com.

Hendrie Weisinger and J. P. Pawliw-Fry, *Performing Under Pressure: The Science of Doing Your Best When It Matters Most*, https://hankweisingerphd.com.

John Zenger, Joseph Folkman, and Scott Edinger, *The Inspiring Leader: Unlocking the Secrets of How Extraordinary Leaders Motivate*, http://zengerfolkman.com.

Kathy Ziola, Communication Works, www.nvctrainingsource.com/kathy-ziola.

Index

About the Author

Michael Gelb is a pioneer in the fields of creative thinking, executive coaching, and innovative leadership. His clients include Emerson, Genentech, Merck, Microsoft, and the Young President's Organization. Michael codirects the acclaimed Leading Innovation Seminar at the Darden Graduate School of Business and also leads seminars for London Business School, the Institute for Management Studies, and Shiv Nadar University in India.

Michael is the author of fifteen books, including the international bestseller *How to Think like Leonardo da Vinci*. Other titles include *Creativity On Demand*, *Innovate like Edison*, *Discover Your Genius*, *Wine Drinking for Inspired Thinking*, and *Brain Power*. His books have been translated into twenty-five languages and have sold more than one million copies.

In 1999 Michael was named "Brain of the Year" by the Brain Trust Charity (other recipients include Stephen Hawking, Garry Kasparov, Ted Hughes, Edward de Bono, and Gene Roddenberry). In 2003 he was awarded a Batten Fellowship by the University of Virginia.

Michael is also a gifted teacher of the Alexander Technique, a fifth-degree black belt in aikido, and a professional juggler who has performed with the Rolling Stones.

www.michaelgelb.com